W9-CBF-738
3 3013 00002 2842

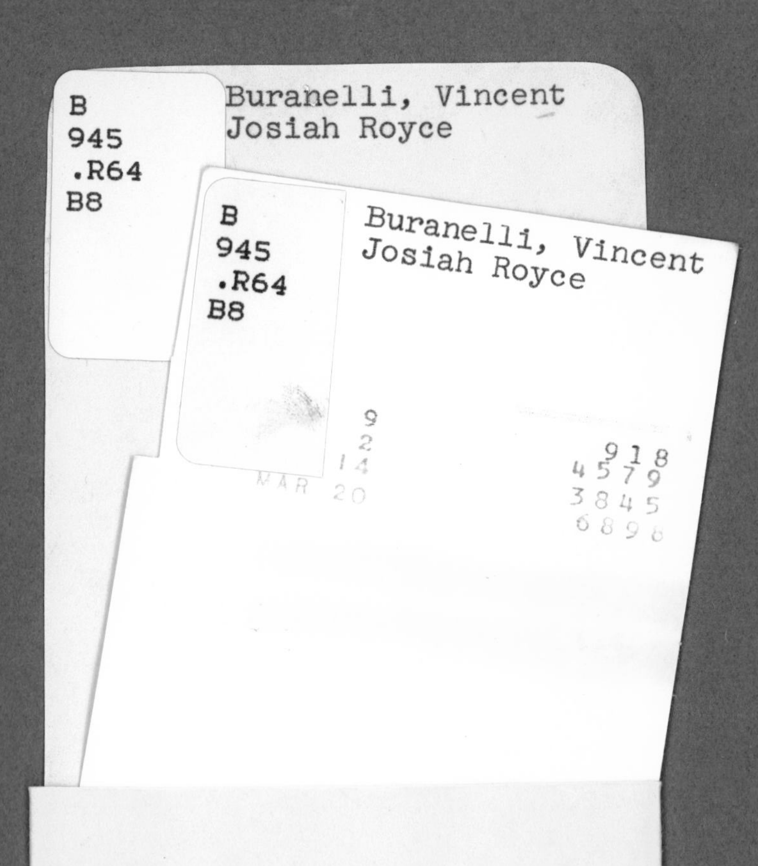
B
945
.R64
B8
Buranelli, Vincent
Josiah Royce
B
945
.R64
B8
Buranelli, Vincent
Josiah Royce

Twayne's United States Authors Series

Sylvia E. Bowman, *Editor*

INDIANA UNIVERSITY

Josiah Royce

TO

MARGUERITE

who did most of the work

Preface

THIS VOLUME is an attempt to present Josiah Royce as he has not been presented before—to describe him in the round and through his multifarious aspects from novelist and literary critic to logician and metaphysician. Since the scope of Twayne's United States Authors Series precludes a full treatment of any single aspect, much less all of them together, the result is an intellectual sketch of Royce rather than an intellectual portrait. Many details are missing; many subtleties of interpretation and alternative explanations are quietly passed over in favor of dogmatic statement. The Roycean metaphysical system is the most obvious case in point, for important books have been devoted to topics that are dealt with here in a few pages, or even paragraphs.

The first two chapters concern the lighter side of the subject. Literature, history, and biography, permitting a faster pace than metaphysics, have the value of introducing Royce's thought without the technicalities of his massive tomes. Chapter I is of special moment to the whole since it deals with Royce as a writer: Without it the rest would not have been worth doing, at least in this form. Chapter II has the interest of a varied life, ranging from the California gold fields of the Forty Niners to post-Romantic Germany and finally to the Harvard adorned by William James.

Since technical philosophy must function as the center of gravity in any discussion of America's great idealist, the next two chapters are devoted to the Roycean system. They form the explicitly philosophical part of the book. Experts on Royce will probably not find anything to interest them in these pages: My intention has been to keep the analysis as simple and logical as possible so that readers without philosophy may be led forward step-by-step into the grand metaphysical theses. In the last chapter comes the summing-up—a backward glance at Josiah Royce to recall the high spots of the path along which he has guided us, and an estimation of his worth as a guide.

A book such as this runs the hazard of being jejune to the professional and confusing to the unprofessional. Breadth of treatment may conflict with depth: If a multitude of facts about the subject are to be given, some can barely be touched; if all the contents are to be completely explained, the latitude may become so narrow as to create serious distortions. And how are exposition and criticism to be balanced in the case of a philosopher who has provoked so much criticism?

My decision has been to mention everything without which there would be a glaring hiatus in Royce's systematic thought; and, where extensive explanations are excluded by the limitations of space, at least to point out either in the text or in the notes just where further research may profitably be pursued.

As for exposition and criticism, I have mingled them in the first three chapters on the assumption that this is the most helpful method. The treatment in the fourth chapter is mainly expository since the first necessity with Royce, as with any thinker, is to find out what he thought and why he thought it. To have inserted criticism after each phase of the argument would have complicated the text and made the book top-heavy. The alternative seemed more appropriate; and so a few salient demurrers to Royce are gathered together in a final sub-chapter which thus becomes not so much an independent piece of criticism as a brief bibliography of the polemical literature wherein may be found the pros and cons.

This intellectual sketch is intended to be an authentic likeness drawn from life, the life of the mind. It might perhaps be subtitled "A Preface to Royce," or, if his own language may be paraphrased with propriety, "The Spirit of Royce."

VINCENT BURANELLI

Princeton, N.J.

Contents

Chronology

1855 Josiah Royce, the son of Forty Niners, is born in the mining camp at Grass Valley, California, November 20.

1866 After receiving his earliest training from his mother, Sarah Royce, he begins his formal schooling in San Francisco.

1871 He enters the new University of California, studies science under Joseph Le Conte and literature under Edward Rowland Sill, reads Mill and Spencer.

1875 Receiving his B.A., he goes to Germany for graduate study at Leipsic and Göttingen; he attends Lotze's lectures on philosophy, reads widely in the German idealistic philosophers and romantic poets.

1876 He enters Johns Hopkins as one of its original fellows, begins to write and teach, hears visiting professor William James.

1878 Receiving his Ph.D., he returns to the University of California as a lecturer in the English department, corresponds with James, publishes "Schiller's Ethical Studies."

1880 He publishes "Shelley and the Revolution."

1881 He publishes *Primer of Logical Analysis for the Use of Composition Students* and "Kant's Relation to Modern Philosophic Progress."

1882 He joins the faculty at Harvard as instructor in philosophy, publishes "Mind and Reality."

1885 He becomes an assistant professor of philosophy at Harvard, refuses to sign the creed for the Lowell Lectures, publishes *The Religious Aspect of Philosophy* and "An Episode of Early California Life: The Squatter Riot of 1850 in Sacramento."

1886 He publishes *California from the Conquest in 1846 to the Second Vigilance Committee in San Francisco: A Study of American Character.*

1887 He publishes *The Feud of Oakfield Creek: A Novel of California Life.*

1888 He visits Australia.

1890 He provokes the controversy with Francis Ellingwood Abbot by publishing "Dr. Abbot's 'Way out of Agnosticism'."

1891 He publishes "Impressions of Australia," "A New Study of Psychology" (a review of James's *Principles*), "The Frémont Legend" and "Montgomery and Frémont: New Documents on the Bear Flag Affair."

1892 He becomes professor of the history of philosophy at Harvard, publishes *The Spirit of Modern Philosophy* and "The Implications of Self-consciousness."

1895 He participates with Le Conte, Howison, and Mezes in the philosophical symposium at the University of California.

1897 He publishes with them *The Conception of God.*

1898 He publishes *Studies in Good and Evil.*

1899 He delivers his earlier Gifford Lectures at the University of Aberdeen, and publishes them under the title of *The World and the Individual, First Series: The Four Historical Conceptions of Being.*

1900 He delivers his later Gifford Lectures, publishes *The Conception of Immortality.*

1901 He publishes his later Gifford Lectures under the title of *The World and the Individual, Second Series: Nature, Man, and the Moral Order.*

1902 He publishes "Recent Logical Inquiries and Their Psychological Bearings" and "The Concept of the Infinite."

1904 He publishes *Herbert Spencer* and "The Eternal and the Practical."

1905 He publishes "Kant's Doctrine of the Basis of Mathematics" and "The Relation of the Principles of Logic to the Foundations of Geometry."

1906 He publishes *Outlines of Psychology,* delivers at Johns Hopkins the lectures published posthumously under the title of *Lectures on Modern Idealism.*

1908 He publishes *The Philosophy of Loyalty, Race Questions, Provincialism, and Other American Problems* and "The Problem of Truth in the Light of Recent Discussion."

1911 He publishes *William James and Other Essays on the Philosophy of Life.*

1912 He publishes *The Sources of Religious Insight* and "The Principles of Logic" in German.

1913 He publishes *The Problem of Christianity,* "An Extension of the Algebra of Logic" and "Relations between Philosophy and Science in the First Half of the Nineteenth Century."

1914 He becomes Alford Professor of Natural Religion, Moral Philosophy, and Civil Polity at Harvard, publishes *War and Insurance* and "The Mechanical, the Historical and the Statistical."

1915 He publishes "An American Thinker on the War."

1916 He prepares *The Hope of the Great Community* for publication. Royce dies in Cambridge, Mass., September 14.

Josiah Royce

CHAPTER *1*

Man of Letters

DESPITE THE FACT that Josiah Royce wrote a readable novel and a mass of highly competent literary criticism, he has never been awarded a niche in the pantheon of American authors. The fame of Royce is that of a philosopher—indeed, *the* philosopher of our cultural history in the sense that he, beyond any other American, set out to be a system-builder of the classical type, gave his allegiance to one of the historic schools of metaphysics,, and defended his metaphysics through many technical volumes with ability, persistence, conviction, and moral energy. It seems never to have been seriously argued that he was also an eminent writer—not unworthy, at his best, of comparison with William James and George Santayana.

Still, Royce began his professional career as an instructor in English; he wrote his first important paper on Aeschylus, and his first book on the means of enhancing literature by the application of logic to grammar and rhetoric; he tried his hand at fiction, some of which was found acceptable for publication; he lectured on numerous occasions before literary societies. If so much of a continuing concern for literature is no proof that he claims some status in belles-lettres, it *is* proof that the question of his literary significance cannot be shunted aside as hardly worth consideration.

Once the question is raised, a little probing brings to light an abundance of material for an affirmative answer. This is no crabbed, inartistic philosophical technician after the model of Charles Sanders Peirce. Royce may not be so virile as James or so elegant as Santayana, but for all that he is the author of some masterly philosophical prose that bears examination beside theirs, while his more explicitly literary efforts throw off sparks of genius not to be found in many better-known American authors of the second rank. Royce the writer is not entirely eclipsed by Royce the metaphysician.

When William James, no inferior judge of prose styles, drew up his essay "On a Certain Blindness in Human Beings," he went to fine literature for eloquent texts with which to adorn his moral. He quotes from the masters: Wordsworth, Tolstoi, Stevenson, Whitman. Among the best of James's selections is the following:

> Pain is pain, joy is joy, everywhere, even as in thee. In all the songs of the forest birds; in all the cries of the wound and dying, struggling in the captor's power; in the boundless sea where the myriads of water-creatures strive and die; amid all the countless hordes of savage men; in all sickness and sorrow; in all exultation and hope, everywhere, from the lowest to the noblest, the same conscious, burning, wilful life is found, endlessly manifold as the forms of the living creatures, unquenchable as the fires of the sun, real as these impulses that even now throb in thine own little selfish heart.

Did we not know the origin of this passage, we might legitimately suspect that it came from Emerson or Whitman. Actually it is from Josiah Royce.[1]

I *The Prose Writer*

Royce himself is largely responsible for the indifference that obscures him as a man of letters. His works, uniformly adept in their conceptual analyses, are very unequal in their literary merits. *The World and the Individual,* his masterpiece, is full of paragraphs marked by the journeyman prose that might have come from the pen of any undistinguished professor of philosophy. This fault is more evident in his highly technical papers, even the titles of which are enough to turn aside the seeker after beauties for the anthology: "Mind and Reality," "An Extension of the Algebra of Logic," "Recent Logical Inquiries and Their Psychological Bearings," "Kant's Relation to Modern Philosophic Progress," and the like.

Anyone who approaches Royce through these papers, supplemented by excerpts from his heavy tomes on the abstractions of reason, will almost infallibly set him down as an important philosopher but no writer of distinction. Most critics *do* so approach him because they are interested in him primarily as a philosopher, and this is the shortest path to the essentials of his metaphysics, to the system of absolute idealism on which his fame as a thinker rests. Hence Ralph Barton Perry's opinion of Royce the writer: "His style was massive and sluggish." [2]

This indictment cannot be allowed to stand. It relies on a foreshortening of perspective that suppresses half the truth, for Royce has two styles, each tailored to a specific audience. When handling logical theorems and categories and transcendentals for the benefit of the professionals of philosophy, he generally chooses to leave ornament to one side and to hammer home his points without worrying about artistic effects. *Then* he can be ponderous and verbose. When his public is wider, when he is writing for the popular magazines or lecturing before laymen, *then* he allows his aesthetic faculty some scope, slackens the tension of his thought with agreeable asides, and writes prose with characteristic felicities. The distinction is that between *Lectures on Modern Idealism* and *The Spirit of Modern Philosophy.*

Naturally there are common elements in whatever Royce touches, and it would be an absurd oversimplification to think that his publications and unedited manuscripts can be neatly bifurcated into the artistic and the inartistic. The rhetorical virtue of clarity is a constant. Royce's high philosophy is inherently difficult, not to be mastered without rereading and rethinking, but his manner of expression is hardly ever an obstacle. The spare scaffolding of his logic allows a firm foothold at every stage from the foundation of the premises to the summit where the implied conclusions await the climber who perseveres. Even his marked tendency to write too much does not compromise this virtue.

Moreover, discourse of any length prompts him to rise occasionally to great rhetoric, to blend art and logic, as in the quotation William James chose from *The Religious Aspect of Philosophy.* The rhetorical dimension of his prose is always available. It is just a question of his taking the trouble to use it. There is no mystery about his success in expounding philosophy to amateurs or his authorship of *The Spirit of Modern Philosophy*, the most engaging history of philosophy ever written in the English language.

Royce, for whom the life of the mind was the really significant thing about any human being, declared to his wife his wish that his biography not be written.[3] Yet he left some fragmentary semi-autobiographical notes, and these by themselves would prove beyond cavil that he had the true literary touch. As early as 1879, when he was still in California, he wrote his "Meditation before the Gate," a vignette in which his poetic nature speaks with a frankness that he would never allow himself again. Communing with his soul, he has no need to curb his expression because of reticence before other men. His spontaneous utterance is suffused with imagination, poetry, subdued emotion, sympathy for nature, and quiet elegiac musing; and his mood could hardly have been captured in words more fitting than these.

> The high dark hills of the western shore of the Bay, the water at their feet, the Golden Gate that breaks through them and opens up to one the view of the sea beyond, the smoke-obscured city at the south of the Gate, and the barren ranges yet farther to the left, these are the permanent background whereon many passing shapes of light and shadow, of cloud and storm, of mist and sunset glow, are projected as I watch from my station on the hillside.[4]

The delicate intimacy of this mood he cannot, from the nature of the case, recapture when he is not himself the subject. His best prose moves into a more restrained key; it is still imaginative, romantic, and earnest, but not so evocative of personal feeling. His sensitivity to nature reappears in *California* and "Impressions of Australia." His eloquence, aroused by poetry, appears in "Shelley and the Revolution":

> To catch a fleeting experience in its marvelous perfection of emotional coloring, to crystallize it and make it eternal, to leave it a jewel in the world's treasure house for all time, that it may flash back in multitudinous rays (how well worn the poor figure is!) the light of all future life that falls upon it—this is the great work of the lyric poet. This Shelley has done, living as he did in the midst of a time of revived emotional life, and has done with a magic power at which we can only mutely marvel.[5]

The dry problem entitled "George Eliot as a Religious Teacher" produces a similar effusion: "Poetry is not always, but yet very often, aptly to be named molten thought, thought freed from the chill of the mountain summits, its crystalline perfection of logical form dissolved, no longer ice, but gathered into tumultuous streams that plunge down in musical song to the green fields and wide deserts of the world where men live, far below." [6]

Of his professional subject, philosophy, Royce writes less ecstatically, for it is impossible to be that moved by metaphysical ideas; but when the context calls for it, he is as brilliant as profound. One of his successful gambits is to bring a lecture on philosophy to life by incorporating into his technical analysis those personal touches that adorn even while they explain.

> *On Kant:* This odd and gentle little man was, as you already see, a singular combination of the keen-witted analyst and the humane lover of all things human. Give him an old problem, or a well-known abstract conception, such as the idea of wisdom or of justice, and he would quickly show you his analytic skill by mentioning a long series of distinctions, of aspects, of possible ways of defining or of stating the thing,—so long a series, and often so dry, that you would at first be likely to suspect him of genuine pedantry. And yet this seeming pedant—what a lover he is of books of travel, of descriptions of live men, and of concrete affairs! [7]
>
> . . . .
>
> *On Fichte:* The true self, therefore (and so far the thing is indeed clear enough), the true self isn't the private person, the individual called Johann Gottlieb Fichte, the impecunious tutor, the wavering lover of Johanna Rahn, the professor in Jena, falsely accused of atheism. The true self, thinks Fichte, is something infinite. It needs a whole endless world of life to express itself in. Its moral law couldn't be expressed in full on any one planet. Johann Gottlieb may be one of its prophets; but the heavens could not contain its glory and its eternal business.[8]

Even when Royce sticks close to the hard abstractions of high philosophy, even then amid merely adequate prose a literary gem may suddenly sparkle forth like a diamond set in brass.

> Survey our life, consider our experience. Look at nature as we men find it. Take account of our temporal and spatial universe. Review the results of our science. In all this you will discover manifold meanings relatively obtained, manifold interrelationships binding together facts that at first sight appear sundered, universality predetermining what had seemed accidental, and

a vast fundamental ontological unity linking in its deathless embrace past, present, future, and what for us seems to be the merely possible forms of Being.[9]

. . . .

Now the one of these two views of Nature—the ancient view of a trivial teleology, and the other, the so-called mechanical conception of nature—is as crudely anthropomorphic as the other. Man's insight into the known laws of Nature is precisely as much due to a struggle with the complexities and irregularities of his experience of Nature, as his industrial arts are due to a conflict with Nature's seeming chaos of climates and of materials. A rigid selection, a long search, and a deliberate rearrangement of the facts offered to us by raw experience, wins, in the one case as in the other, not with any *a priori* certainty, but at times, and to a limited extent, and by virtue of our skill and patience. Nature, as we empirically know it, just as truly seems to resist our efforts to explain the phenomena, as in certain regions it permits us to win. When we win, when we explain and predict, doubtless that is indeed because external Nature is in itself such as to permit us to do so. But the same Nature permits us to find the clay and the coals and metals.[10]

Throughout this prose there is a nice balance of logic and rhetoric: The long sinewy sentences, marching by way of concatenated sub-clauses, parallel the intricate operations of the mind as it pushes along the winding road of philosophical theory. The union of thoughts and words is admirably carpentered. Royce wields, at times like these, an instrument admirably suited to his purposes; and, to use a figure that he might have invented for his own lexicon of expressions, it provides a good example of literary teleology—the adaptation of means to ends in literature. Royce could be, when he chose to be, as artistic a literary teleologist as Bradley.

If Royce writes elaborate paragraphs and pages noteworthy for their interconnected grammatical architecture, he is no less proficient at the shorter form—at the few words that fix the attention of the reader and linger in the memory. Royce is a master of the great line:

The constant student of philosophy is merely the professional musician of reflective thought.[11]

. . . .

> The idea of the moral burden of the individual seems, to many cheerful minds, austere; but, if it is grave and stern, it is grave with the gravity of life, and stern only as the call of life, to any awakened mind, ought to be stern.[12]
>
> . . . .
>
> The incompleteness of *Faust* is the incompleteness of modern thought.[13]
>
> . . . .
>
> It is a great thing to undertake to comprehend the essence, the form, the implications, the meaning, of human ignorance.[14]
>
> . . . .
>
> Endurance is noble because it includes a voluntary defeat of our unwillingness to endure.[15]
>
> . . . .
>
> The liar is a man who deliberately misplaces his ontological predicates.[16]
>
> . . . .
>
> Our duty is to watch and fight, ever on the look-out for foes, as a tiger in the jungle that the hunters are beating might wander, still brave and confident, but ever looking this way and that for the gleam of the bright spears.[17]

Each of these great lines affords Royce a point of departure for expatiating on a critical element of modern thought, of *his* thought. Descending from this rarefied intellectual atmosphere to the warmer level of personal friendship, he wrote a moving tribute to his old comrade, Professor Joseph Le Conte, and brought it to an end with a line of pure peotry: "Among his beloved mountains it was his lot to die."[18]

Any man who could excogitate *pensées* like these was not well served by the otherwise laudatory George Herbert Palmer, whose testimonial to his late colleague registers this verdict on Royce the writer: "Condensed, brilliant, epigrammic writing was never his."[19] If the adverb had been "seldom," the judgment would have been more just.

William James was nearer the mark when, referring not to sentences or paragraphs but to Royce's works as massive wholes, he called Royce "the Rubens of philosophy. Richness, abundance, boldness, color, but a sharp contour never, and never any *perfection.* But isn't fertility better than perfection?"[20]

Had Royce always written in his finest style, to argue for his place in American literature would be superfluous. The argument is necessary because, unlike James and Santayana, Royce is not an artist incapable of declining into inferior prose. He is an artist capable of rising into great prose.

II *The Literary Critic*

Royce became a literary critic for the same reason that he became a logician: Literature and logic helped him master philosophy. He doubtless would have dabbled in both because he had a taste for them, but it was not mere good fortune that the lines he traversed happened to lead him invariably, as if by a compass bearing, back to metaphysical idealism. He refused to busy himself at length with writers or logicians who preached a different moral, whose insights could not be deflected toward his own thinking.

His favorite authors are the sign of his attitude toward letters: He prefers Aeschylus to Sophocles, Goethe to Shakespeare, Shelly to Keats, Browning to Tennyson. This list, clearly, does not imply the superiority of his preferences, for, to take the obvious case, he would not have ranked Goethe above Shakespeare on the score of pure literary genius. Goethe claimed a greater share of his attention because *Faust* taught him more about philosophical wisdom. For this same reason Royce can take delight in lesser poets—in Swinburne, for example, and even in the now-forgotten Edward Rowland Sill, who headed the English department at the University of California when Royce was an instructor on the faculty.

Looking at Royce the literary critic from the other side, from the negative side of the masters he does *not* take the trouble to analyze, he makes little of Dante, Milton or the classical dramatists of France because they do not offer him support for his type of philosophy. Where Royce fails to recognize a reliable guide, he will part company with the most sublime poet; he will abandon any direction that points toward a destination other than his.

While, therefore, it is proper to call Royce a "literary critic," he cannot be measured according to the definitions that apply to Poe, Lowell, and T. S. Eliot. He does not invoke strictly literary canons in order to judge a given work, and he stands at a far remove from Poe's beloved principle of art for art's sake. He ignores the analysis of verse forms, sentence structure, imagery, symbolism, and the other aesthetic counters with which the game of evaluating authors is customarily played. He rather resembles Emerson, examining literature more for lofty ideas than for literary excellence per se. Royce admires great argument more than great language; he is repelled by excellence in handling words when they are the vehicle for false, debased, or paltry ideas.

Royce understood as well as anyone that poetry has standards of its own, and he makes these standards the sole criterion when he compares Shelley and Swedenborg: "Shelley's mysticism is, however, unlike Swedenborg's, purely poetical, and hence perfectly safe, being judged altogether by the standards of emotional truth."[21] This is, for Royce, the lighter side of criticism. He is not really interested in Shelleyan poetry except to the extent that it implies, in Royce's opinion, Roycean metaphysics. *His* Shelly is the Shelly of *Prometheus Unbound,* where "The keenest sense of the real problems of life pervades every line.[22]

The rationale of his criticism comes out more sharply in his handling of Tennyson. Discussing *Locksley Hall* as the poet first wrote the poem and as he revised it many years later, Royce considers the revision a better work on the ground that "if artistically inferior, [it] is ethically higher, and for this reason more satisfying."[23]

What all this means is that Royce, like Plato and Shelly, visualizes poetry and philosophy as bearing on the same truths: Poetry discovers them in sudden flashes of visionary insight; philosophy patiently uncovers them through disciplined ratiocination. The passion of the poet is not at all irrelevant to the cold categories of the philosopher; or rather, the philosopher who fully understands his categories understands that they are vibrant with the life to which the poet is so delicately attuned. The following passages, one referring to poetry and the other to philosophy, reveal Royce's method of making these human enterprises allies rather than strangers.

> *On Shelley:* When people speak of Shelley as preeminently a lyric poet, they commonly neglect to notice what profound consequences for his whole character, as a teacher of truth, are implied in this statement.[24]
>
> . . . .

> *On Hegel:* People usually call Hegel a cold-hearted system-maker, who reduced all our emotions to purely abstract logical terms, and conceived his Absolute solely as an incarnation of dead thought. I, on the contrary, call him one who knew marvelously well, with all his coldness, the secret of human passion, and who, therefore, described, as few others have done, the paradoxes, the problems, and the glories of the spiritual life.[25]

There is something attractive about a critic who reads Shelley for ideas and Hegel for passion. To do so was not a beguiling oddity with Royce. He expands the Shelley-Hegel equation into a whole theory in which poetry enlightens philosophy, and philosophy systematizes poetry.

> Literature often bears to philosophy in general and yet oftener to Ethical Philosophy, the relation of fountain to stream. What the poet suggests about the meaning and the obscurity of life, the ethical philosopher makes the subject of a formal study. The poet sees a tragedy of destiny; and the philosopher makes of it a problem in dialectics, where words war instead of souls. Certainly the stream in this case rises no higher than the source. No ethical system, unless it be the work of a philosopher who is himself a poet, will be found to have in it more insight into life than poetry has already suggested.[26]

Because of this conviction, Royce is as likely as not to begin a philosophical disquisition with an excursion into poetry. That is why he is able to transfer a whole section on poetry from his *Fugitive Essays,* where he is talking about the poets, to his rigorously intellectual *Religious Aspect of Philosophy.*[27]

His philosophical studies reinforced and made permanent the natural bent of his mind toward literature. As a student in Germany during the 1870's, he found philosophy and letters intimately united, the era just past having been one of philosophers who were great writers (Schelling, Schopenhauer) and of poets who were great thinkers (Goethe, Schiller). That is, Royce inherited the Romantic movement of Germany in its multifarious creative aspects, and he plunged into it with the high enthusiasm of youth and genius. He was in Germany to learn philosophy; he devoted his leisure hours to reading widely in literature. Many years later he told a group of his admirers: "I should confess to the charge of having been, during my German period of study, a good deal under the influence of the Romantic School, whose philosophy of poetry I read and expounded with a good deal of diligence."[28]

Royce came back from Germany a convinced romantic of the Germanic persuasion. Throughout his works are to be found the romantic traits that he catalogued with admiration when writing of the poets and philosophers he studied thus early in his career: soaring imagination, bold metaphysical reason, moral earnestness, a craving to find unity in the bewildering flux of sensations, a determination to follow ideals doggedly into every corner of experience, even into religious mysticism and the odd vagaries of pathological psychology. Romanticism is with him more strongly at the beginning than at the end, for he saw with increasing clarity that its vaulting ambitions had to be tempered and regularised with mathematical logic and laboratory science. But the basic imprint on his personality is never effaced. Noble passions never cease to move him as profoundly as noble thoughts.

Much of the chastening rigor with which Royce would control Romanticism was also a gift of his German period, a gift which he acknowledges in his essay on literature as art and science. He notes in "A Neglected Study" that learning at Göttingen and Jena and Heidelberg had come to mean something more than pedantry. Philology and criticism had joined hands. Texts were being established by means of an exact apparatus of scholarship; they were also being read for the same delight offered by the latest books off the press. Men like Mommsen, Zeller, and Wilamowitz-Moellendorf were the reverse of the dry-as-dust professor. They were at once scholars and humanists, and as such they were able to rise to an understanding of the Greek or Roman spirit from which ancient literature emerged as one of its creative manifestations.

Royce's "neglected study" is just this kind of literary criticism applied to modern literature, specifically to English literature. He laments the fact that the field is preempted by the pedants on the one side and by the undisciplined aesthetes on the other, neither being able to understand the national psychology of the people who produced the writers:

> How much is yet to be done in the way of a genuine history of the life and thought of the English people! How little does a student who, like myself, occasionally needs for professional purposes special instruction as to the history of the great English

> Moral Ideas and Ideals, find to aid him in our libraries! Essays of fragmentary and capricious literary criticism, ambitious failures like the magnificently planned and hopelessly unsuccessful book of Taine, numberless biographical sketches, of every degree of power and skill, large collections of raw material, and finally elaborate parasitical growths such as the mass of literary industry that has grown up at Shakespeare's expense: such are the treasures of wisdom that offer themselves to whoever seeks for light as to the evolution of English Literature in its wholeness.[29]

That Royce took his ideal in more than an abstract sense is proven by his endeavor to make it concrete in his analysis of the Romantic movement. He never wrote a full treatise on Romanticism. He never concerned himself with more than a few basic elements of the mental climate that had settled over Europe during the century before his birth. To penetrate the psychology and philosophy latent in its literature was, nevertheless, his ideal, and such was the task that he assumed again and again with zeal and determination. Romanticism occupied his thoughts over the years: "Schiller's Ethical Studies" (1878), "Shelley and the Revolution" (1880), "Pessimism and Modern Thought" (1881), "The Decay of Earnestness" (1881), *The Religious Aspect of Philosophy* (1885), *The Spirit of Modern Philosophy* (1892), *Studies of Good and Evil* (1898).

Agreeing with Matthew Arnold's postulate about great literature being a "criticism of life," [30] Royce endeavors to see how the Romantics criticized life. He confines his research mainly to the Germans (they being the masters of the Romantic mood and the ones he knew best) with side-glances at English literature. Goethe appears as the universal genius of the movement. Schiller ranks just below him, followed by Novalis, Heine, Kleist, and others. For the British, the key names are Byron, Tennyson, Wordsworth.

The picture that Royce sees is, in general terms, this. With Schiller, Romanticism chafes at the limitations of human nature in the grip of natural law, until Kant points to the solution ("Schiller's Ethical Studies"). With Shelley, it demands rebellion in the name of the ideal; promises a speedy advance to human freedom, dignity, and happiness; and luxuriates in passion and mysticism ("Shelley and the Revolution"). With Byron, it would live life to the full in a riot of intense anarchic individualism

("Pessimism and Modern Thought"). Over all thunder the echoes of the Storm and Stress period; and disillusion is frequently the moral of an idiotic tale.

> *On Schiller:* From first to last his motto seems to be that nothing is too earnest for the earnestness of life, and nothing relating to life too barren for the transforming hand of poetry.[31]
>
> . . . .
>
> *On Byron's Don Juan:* It is a mountain stream, plunging down dreadful chasms, singing through grand forests, and losing itself in a lifeless gray alkali desert.[32]
>
> . . . .
>
> *On Tennyson:* The old man thinks gray thoughts, for he is gray, but not all his thoughts are of death.[33]
>
> . . . .
>
> *On the Romantic ideal:* The genius must wander like a humming bird in the garden of divine emotions.[34]
>
> . . . .
>
> *On the verse of the movement:* Emotion tinged with speculative reflection results in the writing of what is called romantic poetry.[35]

One writer stands apart from and above the rest, at once a Romantic and much more than a Romantic. Goethe is for Royce the spokesman of life itself, the supreme union of thought and feeling, the greatest of those who offer a "criticism of life," the widest-ranging mind that ever produced poetry of the highest kind: "*Faust* is the crown of modern poetic effort." [36] As Kant is fundamental for Royce in philosophy, so is Goethe in literature. *Faust* is the analogue of the *Critique of Pure Reason.*

Im Anfang war die Tat—"In the Beginning was the Deed." This powerful line moved Royce at every reading of the poem, and he devoted himself to working progressively deeper into the meaning. He saw that Goethe was not speaking of mere power, or of the emotional thrust of the will into any kind of action, but rather of human effort springing from intelligent purpose. Goethe, by exalting doing above feeling and by giving his thought a philosophical cast, helped Royce to develop an activist metaphysics.

Among the persistent problems of Royce's philosophy is the problem of time. Royce thought that if the relations of past, present, and future, and the relation of all three of eternity, could be given a definitive analysis, most of metaphysics would be established, by implication if not directly. Goethe may have put the germ of this idea in his mind.

Goethe's Faust does not sell his soul to the Devil. His contract with Mephistopheles, no surrender with a time limit, is a wager on his ability to save his soul through a test of character and endurance. The bargain is that he will lose should he ever be tempted into asking that the present moment be extended for his enjoyment. His fate hangs on his undeviating will to effort and to accomplishment rather than to repose.

> *Werd' ich zum Augenblicke sagen*
> *Verweile doch! du bist so schön!*
> *Dann magst du mich in Fesseln schlagen,*
> *Dann will ich gern zugrunde gehn!*
>
> Should ever I to the present moment say
> Pause awhile! you are so fair!
> Then may you fasten me in chains,
> Then will I gladly accept my ruin!

Royce felt that in these tremendous words, inspired poetic genius reached the ultimate perception of essential philosophical truth. His own analysis of the self in time can be understood as a metaphysical commentary on Faust's wager. Since that analysis leads into most of his system, *Faust* is a companion piece to absolute idealism as Royce understood it.

With Goethe as his guide, Royce found his way out of pure Romanticism, for the Romantic cult of emotional irrationalism could not live with the wisdom of making reasoned achievement rather than subjective feeling the end of man. Royce realized that Goethe's personal philosophy of life was far beyond everyone except the most highly favored spirits; but that merely strengthened his admiration and wonder that such a phenomenon had appeared among men.

> The Storm and Stress Period had been full of the thought that there is something grand in the emotional nature of man, and that this something must be cultivated. Now, Goethe, absorbed

> in the faith of the time—himself, in fact, its high priest—learned after a while that all these much sought treasures of emotion were there already, in his own being, and that they needed no long search, no storming at all. He had but to be still and watch them. He needed no anxious brooding to find ideals; he went about it quietly, meeting the ideal everywhere. The object of search thus attained, in so far as any mortal could attain it, Goethe the poet was in perfect harmony with the Goethe of practical life; and so was formed the creed of the greatest man of the century.[37]

Royce's interpretation of Goethe shows most clearly how his literary criticism parallels his philosophical criticism. He admired literature that is infused with thought, philosophy that is infused with passion. That is why the Romantic movement meant so much to him. He wanted to get back to its enthusiasms so that the chill might be taken off the frosty mathematical science that had replaced Romanticism as the dominant cultural forced in the world. He hoped that pedantic scholarship might be vitalized in the same way.

But he would not give up the rigor of abstract thought. Romanticism as such was too "wayward" for him,[38] leading as it did to the excesses of Byron and the despair of Kleist. Early in his career he decided to limit emotionalism with reason in the manner of Goethe. Later in his career he limited it further with symbolic logic. Restrained Romanticism was his ideal at all times.

His desire for a satisfactory synthesis of poetic passion and rigorous intelligence provoked some of his best literary criticism. True, it narrowed his scope, confining him to those writers most susceptible to his technique and causing him to ignore the rest. The technique, nonetheless, applies to some of the greatest masters of literature, and is capable of presenting their work in fresh and fruitful interpretations.

Browning is a case in point. When Royce lectured on *Paracelsus* before the Boston Browning Society, he gave his audience one of the most acute analyses ever made of that difficult masterpiece. The subject was tailored to Royce's method, motivated as the poem is by the interrelation of love and knowledge, and with a reputed wizard for its central character. Browning's Paracelsus is a mystic who believes in private intuition and the subjective grasp of transcendental truths during flashes of enlightenment.

He is also a man fascinated by empirical knowledge, in fact a physician by profession. So here we have that passionate thought, or reasoned emotion, on which Royce placed so high a value.

Or so it seems. As the criticism unfolds, Royce gradually brings to the surface the tragic flaws of character that impel Paracelsus toward his failure and his doom. His mystical emotion is not poetical insight into objective truth: It is whim, if not delusion. His empirical research is not science: It is occultism, with all the vagaries implied by the term. No fusion of the two takes place at the highest level, nor could it have since they are antithetical ways of understanding reality. They are not complementaries but rivals as they take turns dominating Paracelsus' search for wisdom.

> Could the Paracelsus of former days but have understood in his time what love meant, could he have but known how all the waves and eddies of human passion, even when they seem farthest from the divine, reveal God as no object in outer nature, however wonderful, can ever do—the occultist would not have aspired in vain! he would have been transformed, as the man of the future shall be, into the artist. This is the final message of Paracelsus, and the meaning of the whole poem.[39]

Paracelsus is no Faust, or at least not Goethe's Faust. Such is Royce's interpretation, one that will help to clarify the poem for those who are puzzled by it.

The Romantics, in Royce's view, were too reminiscent of Paracelsus, too inclined to revel amid a welter of sensations without direction, of objects coerced into occult monstrosities. Schiller, Byron, and their like have to be improved upon before they become useful. This applies to the technical philosophers of the movement as well as to the poets, and that is why Royce could never be a believing Hegelian despite his admiration for that most romantic of metaphysical masterpieces, Hegel's *Phenomenology of Mind.* It partook too much of Romantic waywardness to satisfy the intellect: "His great philosophical and systematic error lay, not in introducing logic into passion, but in conceiving the logic of passion as the only logic; so that you in vain endeavor to get satisfaction from Hegel's treatment of outer nature, of science, of mathematics, or of any coldly theoretical topic."[40]

Romanticism and anti-Romanticism balance in Josiah Royce the literary critic: The young Royce was mainly concerned to vitalize philosophy with poetry; the older Royce was mainly concerned to systematize philosophy with logic; but young or old, he read and criticized fine literature for pleasure as well as for philosophical understanding.

III *The Historian*

Among the more graceful products of Royce's pen are his writings on history. If he is no Parkman or Prescott, he is no insignificant figure in the history of American historiography. His one large volume in the field is the best chronicle of California ever written; and, when it was reissued in 1948, its publication was more than a pious tribute to the author's memory. The first edition of 1886 remains a standard history.

There is nothing exceptional about an idealist metaphysician devoting his attention to the experience of man in the mass and down through the dusty processes of the temporal order. Royce had before him the lordly example of Hegel, who pursued the activities of his Absolute, not into some Platonic heaven out of space and time, but into the development of cultures and civilizations and the triumphant course of conquerors across the stage of the world.

The mystery about Royce the historian is why so little of Hegel's Romantic enthusiasm for the ancient and the medieval rubbed off on him. Given Royce's interest in Hegel and his excursions into history, given also his talent for the vast synthesis of ideas, we would expect him to rival Spengler his contemporary, or to anticipate Toynbee and Collingwood who came after him. General history would have underpropped Royce's philosophy in the Hegelian fashion (as it did for the more strictly Hegelian Collingwood); for, even confining his thought to one American state, he is able to read many Hegelian morals in his story.

The subtitle of his book tells us that it is not a mere record of men and events: *California from the Conquest in 1846 to the Second Vigilance Committee in San Francisco* is also *A Study of American Character*. It is actually more than that. It is a study of *human* character, an analysis of what happens to men and women who are struggling to produce a stable communal life out of near anarchy. California is a sociological laboratory in which Royce sees the fate of man as a social animal distilled to its quintessence. The concluding paragraph of *California* is as Hegelian as anything in Royce's philosophical works:

> After all, however, our lesson is an old and simple one. It is the State, the Social Order, that is divine. We are all but dust, save as this social order gives us life. When we think it our instrument, our plaything, and make our private fortunes the one object, then this social order rapidly becomes vile to us; we call it sordid, degraded, corrupt, unspiritual, and ask how we may escape from it forever. But if we turn again and serve the social order, and not merely ourselves, we soon find that what we are serving is simply our own highest spiritual destiny in bodily form. It is never truly sordid or corrupt or unspiritual. It is only we that are so when we neglect our duty.[41]

Royce limited himself to California when he could have exploited this thought much more effectively with examples from the past of Greece and Rome, of Europe and America. He never took the interest in general history that he took in general literature. It is doubtful that he would have become a historian at all had he not been fascinated by the American West Coast as he knew it and as he heard about its recent past from his older contemporaries.

This granted, it is no reflection on Royce as historian; it is no warning against superficial or slipshod history. Being Royce, he made himself one of the most thorough and reliable scholars in the field. He read treatises, monographs, newspapers, and a mass of unpublished documents. He put much exact research into articles like "An Episode of Early California Life: The Squatter Riot of 1850 in Sacramento" (1885), "The Frémont Legend" (1891), and "Montgomery and Frémont: New Documents on the Bear Flag Affair" (1891). He wrote so well and so perceptively about his native state, he was so obviously its leading intellectual, that editor Horace Scudder invited him to contribute a full history to the series called *American Commonwealths*. Royce accepted, set to with his usual industry, and handed in a manuscript that satisfied the editor. *California* satisfies us today. It reads better than almost any other volume in the series.

Most of Royce's historical writings are about one subject—the manner in which Mexican California turned into American California. He is the annalist of a conquest. He is the analyst of the results of that conquest. He is the philosopher of what happened, what might have happened, and what ought to have happened. His history, therefore, begins and ends with value judgments. *California* is a moral tale. Royce, sensitive as always to the drama of life, knew that he had a scintillating spectacle to work with. He brings out the drama as he moves from the old Spanish ways of the native Californians, through the fury of the gold rush, and on to the Barbary Coast out of which modern San Francisco was born. He never forgets, notwithstanding, that he is describing men and events highly susceptible to ethical verdicts; and he delivers verdicts with the finality of the San Francisco Vigilantes dealing with a band of horse thieves.

Royce was a patriotic historian who found his fellow countrymen guilty. He would unveil the iniquities of the Americans precisely so that they might learn about themselves and profit from their mistakes, vices, and crimes. "The story," he says, "is no happy one; but this book is written, not to extol our transient national glories, but to serve the true patriot's interest in a clear self-knowledge and in the formation of sensible ideals of national greatness." [42]

He was too knowledgeable about human nature and the historical facts to imagine that he could paint his entire picture in black and white. He explicitly recognizes that the native Californians, while brave, hospitable, and humane, were incurably afflicted with indolence, weakness, pride, poor judgment, and an inability to govern themselves. He commends the Americans for energy, efficiency, good humor, and a genius for establishing political forms in the midst of turbulent disorder. He agrees that, fearing a British or French coup on the West Coast, the American desire to seize California was "inevitable." [43]

But he balks at acknowledging this list of psychological and sociological facts as justification for the conquest; and when he comes to the way the conquest was carried out, he rises in righteous indignation to call it a case of "The Wolf and the Lamb." With caustic irony and sardonic wit he dissects the Bear Flag revolt, which the Americans began by indulging in the genial practice of horse stealing, and which they ended by preaching about American magnanimity to bewildered Californians whose land and persons they had seized. Nothing is more objectionable to a moralist than inverted moralism; and William Ide, who specialized in this form of humbug, has never been handled more fittingly than by Josiah Royce.

> One can but speak for oneself, and, for my part, if ever I hear in future of our great national mission on this continent as civilizers of the Spanish American peoples, if ever I find that this mission has come once more, as it surely some day will come, to the surface of our vainglorious national consciousness, I shall be able to think of nothing but poor Ide, the self-appointed Yankee captain of a chance crowd of marauders, standing benevolently in the "calaboose," before the forty or fifty innocent and imprisoned citizens of Sonoma, and feeling in his devout kindliness that he does God service while he bellows to them an unintelligible harangue, "not a twentieth part interpreted," about man's inalienable rights to liberty and equality, and while he concludes with a reference to Washington, believing himself, meanwhile, to be the Father of the Bear Flag Republic.[44]

As Royce runs down the roll call of Americans involved, he finds that consul Thomas Larkin "is the only American official who can receive nearly unmixed praise in connection with the measures that led to our acquisition of California."[45] The rest appear as faces in a rogues' gallery. Royces depicts them with short trenchant strokes like these:

> *Robert Semple.* Now Dr. Semple became, as fortune would have it, the Thucydides of the Bear Flag War. If one objects to this assertion that in fact there was no real Bear Flag War, only some pillage and skirmishing, we should, indeed, have to admit the objection, but should, in reply, leave it to the reader to modify accordingly his conception of the Thucydides.[46]
>
> . . . .
>
> *Commodore Stockton.* To be sure, he was not very malicious. He did not want to oppress the Californians, when once he should have conquered them. He only wanted his fun, as a gallant and glory-seeking American officer, out of the business of conquering them.[47]

A great crime needs a great criminal. The American conquest of California had its villain of the piece, according to Royce, in one of the distinguished Americans of his time. Throughout this history runs the subplot (in every sense of the word) of John Charles Frémont.

Royce, who interviewed the legendary Pathmarker of the West and unsuccessful candidate for President, and who expressed gratitude for the cordial reception Frémont gave him in Washington, seems to have contracted an *idée fixe* about Frémont's malignity in 1846. He may have been right, but he could have tarnished the image of the idol in many fewer pages than he devoted to the task; and had he done so, he would have left his own image less tarnished.

Although magnanimous by nature, Royce was human enough to be unfair and wrongheaded on a couple of occasions—when he reviewed Francis Ellingwood Abbot's *The Way out of Agnosticism,* and when he described John Charles Frémont's career in California. In both cases he set himself up as a moral arbiter. In the case of Frémont he tripped over the stumbling block that lies close to the foot of every moralist: Hastening beyond the evidence in order that malevolence might not go unpunished, he found blatant iniquity where others less high-minded than himself have been unable to see anything worse than misjudgment; and he denied to himself the good sense that would have dictated a better attempt to weigh the evidence impartially.

He pursues Frémont with implacable rancor, never giving him the benefit of any doubt, never allowing him to appear in a favorable light. Royce contemptuously brushes past Frémont's expressed fears of English intervention and the Mexican army—but without noting that, even if those fears *were* groundless, the fact might not have been so evident to a commander in the field, amid the sound and fury of a revolution, as it was to a scholar looking back from a vantage point atop a mountain of documentary evidence accumulated during forty years.

As Royce fits together the pieces that cohere into a portrait of a blundering knave, he is oblivious to one salient characteristic of his evidence—the element of doubt and mystery that infuses so much of it. Motives being notoriously difficult to judge, especially in retrospect, it was unnecessary to consider Frémont a liar, even granted that his subsequent testimony did not appear consistent with his earlier actions. He might have forgotten what his exact intentions had been when he received word of the Bear

Flag outburst; or his intentions might have been confused, as one would expect of a military man reacting pragmatically to a civilian uprising. At this point Royce's knowledge of psychology ought to have interposed a veto over unqualified judgments.

But then his ethical sense should not have permitted him to make the startlingly incongruous disclaimer: "And I have meanwhile the perfect consolation of knowing that the personal reputation of a distinguished public man such as is General Frémont, who has been a household name in our nation for a generation, is quite independent for good as well as for evil of what I may happen to choose to write here." [48] The reader would have thought that to ruin Frémont's reputation was precisely Royce's intention; and were Royce's words the last word, Frémont's reputation would indeed lie in ruins. It does not do so only because other historians have corrected the Roycean version of Frémont.

Corrected—but not displaced. In its broadest terms the anti-Frémont case put forward by Royce is, if not irresistible, at least plausible. The issue hinges on the famous ride of Lieutenant Archibald Gillespie, who caught up with Frémont at Klamath Lake and delivered to him some messages, written and oral, from Washington, D.C. The historians are still debating whether or not Frémont was instructed by his superiors to begin military operations in California, should he deem it advisable in the interests of the United States. Frémont told Royce that the answer was affirmative; Royce decided that on the evidence it could only be negative.[49] Since Royce held the opinion that the American resort to force was both a blunder and a crime and since he held Frémont personally responsible, his condemnation followed as a matter of course.

Frémont's penetration into the California turmoil, in Royce's view, "was once for all a pure aggression, and there will never again be a chance of making it appear otherwise." [50] It was the gratuitous application of force to a people who, since they would be future citizens of the United States, ought above all to have been conciliated. It was a "rash and in its consequences most disastrous act" that made immeasureably more difficult the subsequent evolution of the two races into a single society.[51]

Today no one doubts that Royce was right about the hostilities of 1846 being a misfortune to everybody concerned. The misfortune may have been the lesser of evils, or an ineluctable historical irony; but there is no proof of this, any more than there is proof of Royce's assertion to the contrary. The least that must be said to the discredit of Frémont is that he seems never to have counseled moderation, or to have understood how much he was adding to the confusion by lending his name and prestige to the violence of his fellow countrymen.

Not all the American leaders were so blind. Thomas Larkin, who had been in California longer than Frémont, and in Monterey where he could comment on events with some authority, instead of in the hills relying on rumor and panic-stricken informants—Larkin believed that the Californians could be persuaded that their self-interest lay in the American connection. Royce had good reason to argue that Larkin rather than Frémont should have been our guide.

If the conquest of California was the original sin, it was not merely the sin of one man, or of the individuals with whom he associated himself at a given moment of history. Royce finds the evils of the period to be symptomatic of the American character in its worst aspect. They were due to "a hearty American contempt for things and institutions and people that were stubbornly foreign and that would not conform themselves to American customs and wishes." [52] The root of the troubled Royce isolates with contrition and sorrow: "The fearful blindness of the early behavior of the Americans in California towards foreigners is something almost unintelligible." [53]

The native prejudice of the invaders was reinforced by greed. Craving the land held under pre-American grants, they soon found reasons that permitted, or rather compelled, them to seize it. The moral law itself would brook no delay on their part: "Providence, you see, and manifest destiny were understood in those days to be on our side, and absolutely opposed to the base Mexican. Providence, again, is known to be opposed to every form of oppression; and grabbing eleven leagues of land is a great oppression. And so the worthlessness of Mexican land titles is evident." [54]

Nothing in the history of his state gives Royce more scope for satire than this kind of thing, and some of his best pages are those that deal with rapacious robbers and petty tyrants who, in manifest good faith, regarded themselves as the very incarnation of generosity, freedom, equality, justice, and various other estimable abstractions.

It is a stern indictment. Yet from the crimes, follies, and misfortunes of the conquest there emerged a viable social order: The state of California arose. There must have been inherent greatness in a people who could produce so remarkable a result from the chaos they had made—and this too is a moral of Royce's history. He was no breast-beating crank unwilling to see the virtues that balanced the vices of his country. He was no philosophical irrationalist for whom the human story must end in fecklessness, brutality, or buffoonery. He does not invoke Hegel to explain the process, but there is a strong suggestion of Hegel's "cunning of the reason" when Royce describes the evolution of California from disorder to unity, from lynch law to justice, from miners' meetings to local government.

This process might also be called "the cunning of the American moral sense." If the conquerors knew how to commit crimes, they also knew how to repent, and moreover how to make their repentance effective in institutional forms. Royce, who placed so much emphasis on society as the creator of freedom and culture and personality, would not deny that the Americans had risen from their moral defeat at the conquest to the triumph of the California in which he was born and nurtured.

> The lesson of the whole matter is as simple and plain as it is persistently denied by a romantic pioneer vanity; and our true pride, as we look back to those days of sturdy and sinful life, must be, not that the pioneers could so successfully show by their popular justice their undoubted instinctive skill in self-government—although indeed, despite all their sins, they showed such a skill also—but that the moral elasticity of our people is so great, their social vitality so marvelous, that a community of Americans could sin as fearfully as, in the early years, the mining community did sin, and could yet live to purify itself within so short a time, not by a revolution, but by a simple progress from social foolishness to social steadfastness. Even thus a great river for an hour defiled by some corrupting disturbance purifies itself merely through its own flow over its sandy bed, beneath the wide and sunny heavens.[55]

Royce was right to subtitle his history of California *A Study of American Character*, for no American can read it without feeling that here is one part of the national ethos writ small. Royce's bad conscience about the conquest of California has but to be enlarged to become America's bad conscience about the conquest of Mexico. Were Royce alive today, he could offer a further expansion of his ethical analysis, and portray the United States confronting its own people and the other peoples of the hemisphere and the world. When he wrote "Some American Problems in Their Relation to Loyalty," he formulated a passage that has not yet lost its relevance.

> Instead of dangerous sectionalism, we now have the other dangerous tendency towards a war of classes, which the labor-unions and many other symptoms of social discontent emphasize. We have that corrupt political life which partisan mismanagement exemplifies. And we have that total indifference to all forms of loyalty which our seekers after individual power sometimes exhibit, and which occasionally appears as so serious an evil in the conduct of the business of certain great corporations.[56]

We want, as Royce wanted, an elevation of standards in the private and public lives of Americans, and a better understanding of our obligations to the international community. Much has been done since his era; much remains to be done. That is why *California,* a magisterial history and a weighty sociological investigation, is a tract for our time.

IV *The Novelist*

Having written a history of California, Royce wrote a novel of California. Having dealt with the real drama of real characters, he passed on to the fictional drama of men and women created by his imagination. The distinction of fact and fiction was actually not very great, for *California* reads like a novel when its most colorful personalities are indulging in their most titillating conduct; and it provided Royce with background material for *The Feud of Oakfield Creek* (1887).

He hoped and believed that his story would enjoy at least as much popularity as his chronicle, an attitude that turned out to be hopelessly over-optimistic when put to the test of the market place. The public remained indifferent. The novel fell stillborn from the press. The author, according to Santayana, reacted with "silent disappointment."[57]

"Victorian melodrama set in Old California" seems as appropriate a pigeon-hole as any for *The Feud of Oakfield Creek,* which too often sounds like Dickens at his worst and Marie Corelli at her best. Perhaps the reader could forgive the fact that jilted Ellen Escott is found dead in the rose garden beneath the window of her successful rival for Tom Eldon's affections. The words of Bertha Boscowitz to Alf Escott are not so easily forgiven: "It's murder that's in your heart, Mr. Escott. Beware of it." [58] Royce flirts with bathos on several occasions before his tale has wound its way to its conclusion. Nor does this kind of feeble humor, which in any case is too little in evidence, offer adequate atonement: "She felt like stout Cortez on the peak in Darien, and gazed with a wild surmise on the ocean of social possibilities that would be open before a girl who should always sew the buttons on her gown." [59]

The surprising thing is that Royce should have employed so few of his literary gifts on his novel. The mood of poetic romanticism that covers so much of his autobiographical, critical, historical and philosophical writing appears only spasmodically and diluted. The prose is almost uniformly below his best, a vice compounded by too much use of the labored past perfect tense. There is an unbelievable ineptitude in his handling of the names Tom, Margaret, and Harold—the author forgetting that "Harold" is actually the surname of his character.

Royce might have done better than this. His romantic qualities fitted him for the building of a world populated by his own creations. He knew his setting at first hand. He had a rhetorical sense that makes him cast philosophical argument into dialogue form whenever to do so seems apposite, and he could have had his characters speak to one another more plausibly. His prose style was adequate, if only he had taken the pains to keep it adequate. Having shaped and defined a good plot, he had no intellectual right to encumber it with so much excess baggage.

Even his metaphysical theory could have been an aid to him. He held that narrative is an especially significant form of writing because it describes the content of time, and so touches one of the fundamentals of reality.

> We watch the moving and tend to neglect the apparently changeless objects around us. And that is why narrative is so much more easily effective than description in the poetic arts;

and why, if you want to win the attention of the child or of the general public, you must tell a story rather than portray coexistent truths, and must fill the time with series of events, rather than merely crowd the space of experience or of imagination with manifold but undramatic details. For space furnishes indeed the stage and the scenery of the universe, but the world's play occurs in time.[60]

Royce had risen to the challenge of drama-through-time when he wrote about realities in *California;* but he did not repeat his triumph when he came to the fiction of *The Feud of Oakfield Creek*. The subtitles alone are evidence that something is wrong, for while the history is genuinely *A Study of American Character,* the story is not what it claims to be, *A Novel of California Life*. It is not romanticized travel literature, or a social biography of a province. Place names are there—San Francisco, Oakland, the Bay, the Contra Costa Hills; the action ranges across them; and yet Royce never pauses for a real topographical description. There is no "feel" of California here, and the background is of so little import to the plot that the characters might be shifted to any other wide-open locale without much loss to the novel. Royce could have enlivened his story had he dropped some of his heavy-handed fiction and plagiarized *California* and "The Squatter Riot" for color.

The vices of *The Feud of Oakfield Creek* are easy enough to tabulate. Still, this is a readable novel with undoubted literary merits. The melodrama is not ineffective in passages like these: "Peter Dover was dead, she said, dead for years and years. Ellen wept at this, and begged once more for the direction, and went off, raving and sobbing, into the darkness and the storm." [61] Or: "The moon rose late over near and rugged hills that night, and, as Harold lay awhile, broad awake, the shadow of the window-sash and the wide-branching, tall, and shapely plants could be seen on the polished wooden floor, just beside one of the rugs." [62]

Although the feeling for nature does not flow out through Royce's pen as it does in his private notes (which is a pity since he enjoyed the poetic license to loosen the controls on his imagination), there is more than a hint of the mood in this paragraph:

The sun was now very near the eastern horizon. The level way wound among the oaks as they rode. It was still vacant, save

> for the two early travelers. A hawk wheeled near them. Two or three horses, that had been wandering in a vast pasture-field by the roadside, looked at them wistfully, as they went by, and neighed softly. In the west, behind the travelers, scattered masses of fog partly hid the summits of the Contra Costa Hills. Mount Diablo loomed up ahead of them, larger than ever.[63]

The psychology of motivation, in however stilted a language it may express itself, is fundamentally credible. The dramatis personae are not pasteboard puppets crudely put together. We can recognize the types they represent. Alf Escott is the well-meaning, self-righteous, impliable, feckless literary man whose most typical advice is: "Never be reconciled to your enemy if he's a man." [64] Alonzo Eldon is the powerful tycoon, the robber baron of the Coast, albeit with a taste for quasi-socialist theorizing. Louis Boscowitz is the villain of the piece, the corrupt editor, the Iago from Central Europe with a penchant for setting others to quarreling. Ellen Escott is the frail sentimental tragic figure; Tom Eldon, the self-pitying traitor and failure; William Harold, the upright honorable man with the makings of a hero, if the story had been allowed a hero; Bertha Boscowitz, the raw-boned, frustrated spinster of moral energy and grand projects; Mrs. Rawley, the prim Victorian clergyman's wife "with a glance that's as solemn as the trump of doom." [65] The strongest and most sympathetic character in the novel is Margaret Eldon—self-possessed, mistress of her emotions, compassionate partner of her conscience, the one integrated personality who understands herself and the rest. These personalities meet, collide, and recoil in a closely meshed web of actions and counteractions.

One thing that must be said for Royce is that he resists the temptation to moralize or to allow his characters to do so. The few times that he interjects himself into the story as commentator, his appearance is appropriate, and once he produces a striking allegory that is worth a moment's interruption of the narrative.

> Vanity and Benevolence are beautiful comrades. They walk gayly side by side, each charmed with the other, each amusing the other by means of an endless wealth of pious lies. It is not until they come to a very deep stream, and try to ford or to swim it, that they part company. For Benevolence, always being, as the

> inferior virtue, a little awkward and clumsy in such crises, is apt to get lost somewhere in the flood. Then the other, after long and hard swimming, has to weep in lonesome and shivering nakedness on the further bank, fruitlessly calling for the old friend, who has sunk out of sight, perhaps forever.[66]

The plot that gives its name to the book is one that will not be unfamiliar to anyone living in the day of the omnipotent Western. This genre had not yet mushroomed into the most successful folklore of the century, but Royce knew the work of Bret Harte, who had held the field ever since the 1860's. Three years before *The Feud of Oakfield Creek* appeared, Helen Hunt Jackson had written a popular success, *Ramona*. Royce could, therefore, hope to capitalize on a trend. (Interestingly, the writer who would really establish the Western with *The Virginian*, Owen Wister, graduated from Harvard a few months before Royce arrived.)

The plot of Royce's Western involves a disputed tract of land ("the long strip that borders Oakfield Creek") and a colony of settlers who, threatened with eviction by a local magnate and speculator, reach for their rifles and announce their determination not to give up their holdings without a fight. The story then moves forward to the showdown, the climax of the book.

What raises *The Feud of Oakfield Creek* above the level of the Zane Grey-Max Brand Western is the tapestry woven by Royce across the frame of this land dispute. He brings forward personalities in conflict with their enemies, with their fate, with themselves. Speculator Alonzo Eldon, representing the Land and Improvement Company, clashes with the spokesman for the settlers, Alf Escott. This conflict is complicated by the old friendship and the more recent enmity of the two men, by Eldon's intermittent but real desire to give the settlers their due, and by the dubious moralities and legalities of the Oakfield Creek claim.

Now Tom Eldon, Alonzo's son, had jilted Ellen Escott, Alf's daughter, in order to marry the wealthy widow Margaret Dover—a circumstance followed shortly thereafter by Ellen's death and by Escott's estrangement from the whole Eldon family. As the story opens, this pathetic tragedy haunts and divides Tom and Margaret as an unexpiated sin, one that Tom would expiate now. To that end he proposes squaring accounts with his victims and his conscience by persuading his father to abandon the Oakfield Creek claim, leaving Alf Escott and the settlers to the peaceful cultivation of their land. Tom Eldon convinces his wife that she ought to act for him with her father-in-law, and in the same way he ropes in a friend, William Harold, to act for the suspicious, touchy, and self-righteous Escott. Naturally the author stirs the cauldron by having Margaret Eldon and William Harold develop a romantic attachment, which, however, in good Victorian fashion, remains entirely innocent.

At this point, enter the villain—Louis Boscowitz. Since Boscowitz is a journalist, it follows that he publishes a scandal sheet, and that one of the "scandals" he digs up, exaggerates, and puts in the worst possible light is the friendship of Margaret Eldon and William Harold. The upshot is a split in the Eldon family. Old Alonzo Eldon, refusing to deal with Harold any longer and too angry to compromise with those Harold represents, leads a posse out to Oakfield Creek to take possession of the land by force. In the shooting affray that follows, both Tom Eldon and Alf Escott are killed. Alonzo Eldon thereupon retreats back to San Francisco, leaving Oakfield Creek to the settlers, and withdraws into the life of a recluse. Margaret Eldon and William Harold might then have married and rung the curtain down on the happy ending toward which so many novels of the Victorian period make their way, but Royce preferred to separate them physically while uniting them spiritually, which in itself amounts to a rather Victorian solution.

This is a strong plot, well reasoned and skillfully wrought. Royce carries the reader on, although at too meandering a pace, from his premise about the start of the feud to its conclusion in the rifle fire along Oakfield Creek. His digressions all contribute to the main theme. His set pieces are often remarkably dramatic, the best being a rattling good story of a fight with the Indians. Neither Harte nor Wister could have improved on the few words in which Royce captures the scene of danger, confusion, and helter-skelter movement:

> It was too long a range, of course, but the shot did the business for us. For thereupon there was shouting, and there came more shots and a general outcry; and some of the mules began to get unruly, and two or three of the mustangs near me reared and plunged; and somebody—I don't know if it was the major or not—

> gave the word, or what sounded like it; and there was dust, and the crushing of sage-brush under foot, and I saw some horses stumbling—and so there we of the front rank were, all charging together, in an irregular sort of line, across the level and up the barren side of the hill.[67]

If Royce had maintained this pace through more of the book, it might have caught the eye of the public. If he had pruned his text and tightened up the story, it might have caught the eye of the critics. The trouble with *The Feud of Oakfield Creek* is that Royce wrote it so fast that it reads too much like a second draft. Yet it deserves to be better known, for it holds the reader who will do a bit of re-editing for himself by judicious skipping. And it has the permanent interest of a novel written by Josiah Royce and dedicated to William James.

CHAPTER 2

The Wandering Philosopher

ALTHOUGH Royce was unwilling to sit for a biographical portrait, no one who hopes to understand him can afford to observe his self-denying ordinance. No philosopher emerges from a vacuum with his system ready-made. Each has a life history without which his abstract thought would probably have been quite different—even Kant, despite a famous *mot* of Heine to the contrary. The Sage of Konigsberg came of a Pietist family, studied the prevalent philosophies of his time, was roused from his "dogmatic slumber" by Hume, wrote his *Critique of Pure Reason*, and did many other things that belong in a biography.

With Royce we have some license to pursue the biographical facts because he himself did so in his personal notes, and again when speaking about the way in which his metaphysics developed. He himself tabulated the influences to which he submitted while his thought was still malleable. Not to follow him at least as far as he went in his "Autobiographical Sketch" would be an intolerable adherence to his precept and violation of his practice. Like any thinker, he becomes easier to follow when he is followed through the genetics of his intellectual evolution, nor should we forget how much importance he attached to that method when expounding other philosophers. His sparkling biographical asides are not mere digressions in his history of philosophy.

There is one other point that should be made about Royce as a subject for biography. He lived an interesting life in interesting places. He clashed not only with ideas but with men, of whom John Charles Frémont was the greatest. He left statements and letters bearing on his odyssey through the world, with enough implications for us to infer much of what is not there. All this is bound to be used. Some day some one is going to write a big volume on the life and times of Josiah Royce; and it will be—if no rival to the spectacular lives of Descartes, Fichte and Russell—at least something to set beside those of Aquinas and Dewey, and much more entertaining than that of Kant.

I *California*

"I am a Californian . . ." So begins Royce's "Meditation before the Gate."[1] It was a theme to which he returned with much emphasis while he was attempting to think back to the origins of his intellectual history; and it meant something more than the popular cliché about the boy being father to the man, or the psychological cliché about the importance of childhood for maturity.

Royce's native state gave him a dramatic start in life. He was born near the gold mines only six years after the Forty Niners had come pouring in through the Sierra Nevadas and around the Horn, only nine years after the end of the turbulent historical period that provided the material for *California*. His background was not the staid New England of James and Peirce, or even the settled frontier city that St. Louis had become by the time the St. Louis Hegelians arrived.

California, recently the scene of conquest and war, still troubled by the legacy of violence, could not be taken for granted in any political or social sense. The brawling days were too near. There was a tension in the atmosphere that forbade naïve attitudes toward communal life, even by a child, certainly one as precocious as Josiah Royce. He was unable to understand the impact on his youthful intelligence at the time, but years later he realized in retrospect just how powerfully California had influenced him. Less than a year before his death, reminiscing briefly at the banquet in his honor, he told of his childhood in Grass Valley in the California gold fields, of his family life, and of the manner in which the idea of a historical past first came to him in an ingenuous, formless awakening of the intelligence. This passage from his "Autobiographical Sketch" is so revealing that it is always quoted:

> My earliest recollections include a very frequent wonder as to what my elders meant when they said that this was a new

> community. I frequently looked at the vestiges left by the former diggings of miners, saw that many pine logs were rotten, and that a miner's grave was to be found in a lonely place not far from my own house. Plainly men had lived and died thereabouts. . . . What was there then in this place that ought to be called new, or for that matter, crude? I wondered, and gradually came to feel that part of my life's business was to find out what all this wonder meant.[2]

The mature Royce, surveying his career as it neared its end, recalled that his childish experience of communal life had started him on the intellectual pilgrimage that ended only when he had reasoned out his sophisticated philosophy of the state. The enigmas had begun to reveal themselves before he left Grass Valley. The solutions that would satisfy him were years and decades away as he gazed, fascinated, at the relics of the turmoil that had so recently shaken his state. The moral of the saga he would draw in the concluding paragraph of *California;* the metaphysical explanation, in his works on the community.

Meanwhile, and before the idea of California had any meaning for him, he was being trained in a moral code no less germane to his later thought. The influence of his mother, whom he admired beyond filial devotion for her character and intelligence, was lifelong. Sarah Royce, one of the neglected women of American history, deserves to be better-known—a statement that will not be denied by anyone who has read her memoir published under the title *A Frontier Lady: Recollections of the Gold Rush and Early California*. This memoir she set down for the use of her son when he was writing his history of their state. He dedicated his book: "To My Mother, A California Pioneer of 1849." He paid her the intellectual compliment of treating her as a trustworthy observer of the California to which she had come as a Forty Niner.

Thousands of anonymous women suffered through the harrowing snailpaced ride by covered wagon across dust and mud and rivers and mountains to the West Coast. Sarah Royce was one of the few articulate enough to leave a written account of the experience; and she does so in words that are dramatic and moving just because the author makes no attempt to be either. Her memoir has served as source material for many scholars, but for none so much as for Josiah Royce.

More than that, it is a clue to her, and his, mentality. Sarah Royce was not just writing autobiography. She was expounding a philosophy of life, a religion to which she went for consolation during the trek. She carried her Bible with her as she jolted onward from Council Bluffs to Eldorado beyond the Sierras, her husband driving and her young daughter beside her on the seat. Every trial, every hazard or mischance, sent her to the appropriate biblical text. Thus sustained, she could not be daunted by loneliness or thirst, or outfaced by Indians or wild animals.[3]

When she arrived in California, she was engulfed in the bewildering flux of a society struggling to rid itself of its excesses, to live down its recent past, to forge a new political entity. It was a scene that provoked her moral sense, just as it would provoke her son's after the agonizing was over. She has comments, not unworthy of being his, on individuals and institutions from the Mother Lode to San Francisco. She estimates church attendance; she evaluates class mores; she offers sober reflections on the fact that married men envied bachelors. Much of this reappears, with credits, in Royce's account of the period.[4]

The unquenchable optimism of her religion, Sarah Royce inculcated on Josiah Royce; and, although the specific tenets of her Protestant and Puritan faith did not retain any hold on him once he had become old enough to question them, her moralistic piety carried over into his personality. His Pauline theology is hers transmuted into more philosophical and less orthodox terms. He says that, while he "very greatly enjoyed my mother's reading of Bible stories," he could not accept her pious observances with her simplicity because "I was a born nonconformist."[5]

After the experience of home, family, and immediate environment, Royce moved into the larger world of school in San Francisco, where his quick intelligence was further sharpened by contact with rowdy schoolboys. This childish confrontation with life gave way to a more distinctly intellectual training when he entered the University of California as an undergraduate. By the time he received his degree in 1875, his understanding had become the powerful instrument that we find in his books, had already begun to meditate on the perdurable perplexities that have beset human thought since the classical Greeks first formulated them in rational terms. Royce has noted for us the intellectual acquisitions that he took with him from the university:

> The principal philosophical influences of my undergraduate years were: 1. the really very great and deep effect produced upon me by the teaching of Professor Joseph Le Conte—himself a former pupil of Agassiz, a geologist, a comparatively early defender and exponent of the Darwinian theory, and a great light in the firmament of the University of California of those days; 2. The personal influence of Edward Rowland Sill, who was my teacher in English, during the last two years of my undergraduate life; 3. The literary influence of Stuart Mill and of Herbert Spencer, both of whom I read during those years.[6]

This record is of interest and importance in the Royce canon because so much of his mature thought, whether pro or con, touches the names he mentions, and can be epitomized with reference to them.

The most potent inspiration of Josiah Royce the undergraduate was his professor of science. Joseph Le Conte had roamed over much of America with a geological hammer in his hand and a philosophy of transformism in his head. Arrived in California, he joined the staff of the recently founded university, of which he quickly became the leading light. Le Conte brought the thrill of scientific discovery to the provincial isolated mentality of the West Coast; he made a moderate international fame with his books; he taught a generation of students who remembered him with respect and gratitude.

Josiah Royce, in his filial memoir written after Le Conte's death, describes the fervor with which he followed his professor's lectures on the earth and its place in the solar system. The scientific problem that stuck most insistently in Royce's memory was that of the composition of the center of the earth. He could think of few better illustrations, when he came to the philosophy of science, than the manner in which Le Conte marshaled facts and hypotheses to support the contention that the center of the earth must be solid, not fluid.

The actual geological theory Royce considered to be of minor importance compared to the process of arriving at it. What Le Conte taught him was *method*—the step-by-step movement of the intellect amid accumulated data, the persistent determination not to reason against the evidence, the waiting for the moment when rational instinct would perceive order where there was only seeming chaos.[7] This instinct is evidently comparable to that of the poet and the artist, as Royce the critic defined it. The difference was that in the science of Le Conte he saw the significance of *controlled* intuition, and it shielded him from any credulous acceptance of the vagaries of the Romantic movement in which he would shortly be immersed.

The professor also gave the pupil a philosophy, or at least the makings of one. Le Conte called himself an "evolutional idealist." By this term he meant that, while he agreed with Darwin on the mutation of species and the descent of man from subhuman ancestors, he could not accept the evolutionary agnosticism of Huxley and Haeckel. To make evolution cohere with idealism rather than with materialism was the purpose of Le Conte's philosophizing. Since Royce later applied himself to the same task, the relevance of the one thinker to the other would be plain, even if we did not have Royce's explicit testimony to it.

When Royce, now a famous professor in his own right, went back to the University of California in 1895 to take part in a symposium on philosophy, Le Conte was one of those invited to speak on Royce's paper. That Le Conte was not so severe as the others (G. H. Howison and Sidney Edward Mezes) followed from more than the old friendship of the two and from more than the fact that Royce prefaced his lecture with a reference to Le Conte, "who first set before me, in living presence, the ideal, still to me so remote, of the work of the thinker. . . ."[8] It followed rather from the fact that Royce, for all his bold departures into metaphysics and mathematical logic, still came out at a philosophical position on which Le Conte could stand without much discomfort.

Their difference at this symposium centered on the question of how far the theory of evolution has a bearing on metaphysics. Le Conte made the development from nebula to man central to his theorizing, and he argued that evolution reveals the essential bond between the temporal and the eternal.[9] Royce, who confessed himself unable to accept so bold an interpretation, restricted evolutionary thought more closely to positive science.[10] The unifying bond between Le Conte and Royce was this: Royce accepted Le Conte's thesis that evoluion, properly understood, necessarily points by implication to an idealist philosophy.

While Royce the undergraduate was learning science and

evolutionary philosophy from Le Conte, he was learning literature and aesthetics from Edward Rowland Sill. He and Sill began on opposite ends of the teacher-pupil educational fulcrum, continued as colleagues in the English department of the University of California, and remained good friends until Sill's death in 1887. Sill was the university's man of letters—poet, prose writer, essayist, critic, aesthetician. Almost all of his opera have long since fallen by the wayside, and his stature today is that of a minor poet in the American anthology.

The primary effect of Sill on Royce lay in the estimation of literature as such. Where Le Conte revealed to this student the relevance of science to the interpretation of experience, Sill impressed upon him the fact that aesthetic appreciation is just as basic. Royce's English course convinced him that belles-letters are not, or ought not to be, a diversion from more important things. His concern for literary criticism began at the university, although Sill's brand of criticism lost its appeal for him. Sill was a technical master of the subject who viewed it from the standpoint of pure aesthetics, from the standpoint of those who look for unique literary values. He analyzes, in the conventional way, words and their suggestiveness, the power of imagery, the function of symbols and music in verse. He says, without the philosophical implications of Royce's somewhat similar judgment, that lyric poetry is the highest form of literature.[11]

The professor was partly responsible for the secession of his pupil from exclusively aesthetic criticism. Sill wrote quasi-philosophical essays, echoes of which can be heard in Royce's later pronouncements. Sill's essays are too superficial to be Roycean, but some of the titles reveal a connection between the two minds: "Individual Continuity," "The Felt Location of the 'I'," "What Do We Mean by 'Right' and 'Ought'?" Royce applied himself to Sill's problems without stopping at Sill's *simpliste* conclusions.

There remained the professor as poet. Perhaps here Royce first appreciated the force of literary expression, for Sill the poet moved him as Sill the prose writer could not. Years later, discoursing on philosophical ethics and making the point that the absurdities of life puzzle us more than its flagrant evils, Royce went to his old teacher, colleague, and friend for a suitable text. Sill's "The Fool's Prayer" appears in *The Spirit of Modern*

Philosophy, and the fifth stanza summarizes the idea under discussion.

> 'Tis not by guilt the onward sweep
> Of truth and right, O Lord, we stay;
> 'Tis by our follies that so long
> We hold the earth from heaven away.[12]

Negligible verse; but Royce was willing to overlook the literary shortcomings for the sake of the philosophical thought. It was the same attitude that he brought to the masters of literature from Aeschylus to Goethe.

While Royce was going through his formal studies at the university, he was beginning to read for himself on the side. Almost as a matter of course, he encountered one of the most famous names extant, Herbert Spencer. It takes some historical imagination to understand why Spencer was so highly esteemed at that time, for today no one reads him except as an academic duty. Royce himself came to hold the English would-be polymath in low regard. But in the 1870's, Spencer was required reading, and doubtless both Le Conte and Sill advised Royce to read him.

There are intimations in Royce's writings that, on a first reading, Spencer threw a spell over him. The *Synthetic Philosophy* was the first example of comprehensive philosophizing to come to his attention, and he felt intoxicated, as undergraduates do, at the grandiose idea of a unifying theory whereby the scattered elements of human knowledge might be brought together, elucidated, and explained. Royce wrote about Spencer:

> Science and religion, empiricism and rationalism, Locke and Kant, egoism and altruism, mechanism and evolution, nature and history,—such are some of the seemingly opposing forces that he would critically reunite, even in the act of dwelling upon their warfare. His world, too, is rent by great conflicts; but its unity is to be more than its conflicts. Mr. Spencer's great popular reputation is largely due to this organizing spirit that everywhere shows itself in his writings. That, again, is why young men love him so intensely. And their love is so far well suggested by his imposing dignity of enterprise.[13]

Josiah Royce was one of these "young men." Grown older, wiser, more experienced, and better read in the philosophical systems, his enthusiasm for Spencer evaporated. He decided that

Spencer's achievement had fallen drastically short of his ambition, that the *Synthetic Philosophy* failed of a genuine synthesis, and that the Spencerian "Unknowable" amounted to a surrender rather than a triumph: "In the same breath Mr. Spencer, in fact, seems to assure you that he knows all and nothing about this unity of scientific truth. The real outer world is according to him this Unknowable itself. The Absolute is an impenetrable mystery. Consciousness cannot transcend its own boundaries. The limitation of knowledge is thus for Mr. Spencer the tragic defeat of the highest purpose of knowledge." [14]

The Spencerian structure proved to be jerry-built when Royce inspected it under the guidance of better philosophers. It had to come down. What lasted was Spencer's perception that *some* structure *had* to be erected: "His demand that evolutionary concepts shall be unified, remains a permanently inspiring logical idea which will bear much fruit in the future." [15]

Royce mentions John Stuart Mill as the second thinker who invigorated his undergraduate lucubrations, but the intellectual relationship is more tenuous than with Spencer. The presumption would be that Royce is referring principally to Mill's *System of Logic,* once the most celebrated work in a field that Royce proceeded to make his own. His first book is largely based on the kind of logic that could have been taken from Mill: *Primer of Logical Analysis for the Use of Composition Students* (1881). By that time Royce had become aware of the post-Mill revolution in logic, and he drew on revolutionaries like Boole and Sigwart; but he found many of the traditional forms of reasoning dating from Aristotle adequate for a textbook, especially one intended for the literary curriculum where there was no question of rarefied advanced thought.

If Royce read very far in Mill's metaphysics during his student days, he did not react favorably to it. The one of its tenets that appears prominently in his volumes on metaphysics is Mill's definition of matter, which is presented as an example of the erroneous theory that reality is what validates ideas: "John Stuart Mill elaborated our Third Conception in his famous chapter on the 'Psychological Theory of Our Belief in an External World,' in his *Review of Sir William Hamilton's Philosophy*. His definition of matter as a permanent possibility of sensation is altogether of our present type." [16]

The refutation of Mill and of those who think as he does is an integral part of Royce's mature philosophy. Royce classes Mill, to this extent, with the critical relationalists who confuse reality and possibility by failing to see that the appeal to validity leaves unaccounted for the realm of truths that are never validated. Royce accepts critical realism as far as it goes, but he intends to go a lot further.

The ethical utilitarianism of both Spencer and Mill can be ignored in the biography of Royce's mind. He had little use for it, although here again he would incorporate whatever truth it possesses into a more satisfactory philosophy.

Royce's California experience forms the background to his thought, and he rightly stressed it as such when he reminisced about the path by which he had arrived at his system. A background is not, however, a centerpiece. To call him a "California philosopher" is more than an exaggeration. His native state did not provide him with his philosophy: He belongs to a school that he would have joined had he been reared and educated in Boston or Oxford or Leipsic. Bradley and Windelband did not have to go to California to become idealists.

Conversely, California could have made Royce an empiricist or materialist. Ralph Barton Perry has analyzed the curious inverse parallel between Josiah Royce and William James—the traditional idealist from the frontier contrasting with the experimental pragmatist from New England, when, by their origins, they might have been expected to contrast in precisely the opposite way.[17] Nor should it be forgotten that Royce lamented to James that there was no philosophy on the West Coast.[18]

California put fundamental philosophical questions into Royce's mind. The answers came to him only when he went abroad to continue his studies.

II *Germany*

With his bachelor's degree in his pocket, twenty-year-old Josiah Royce betook himself to Germany in the fall of 1875, making what was already an orthodox pilgrimage for Americans in search of higher education. James had been there a few years before; Santayana would arrive a decade later; and the numbers are past counting of those who sailed from America during the late nineteenth century to find a new world of thought beyond the Rhine. The graduate schools of Germany were the admiration of the West. They were the model according to which those of American universities were set up by educators who had gone through the mill of the German professorial and tutorial systems.

This pro-Teutonic attitude prevailed until the outbreak of World War I. The British universities were considered by Americans to be too class-ridden, too devoted to the production of gentlemen rather than scholars. It was an ideal that could be admired, but could not be imitated. The French universities, on the contrary, seemed too literary: They cultivated quick wit and fine prose, which again defied imitation across the Atlantic.

Germany was exactly what American students and educators were looking for. In the land of Bismarck and the Kaiser, but also of Kant and Brahms and Ranke, they found scholarship linked to a personal tradition of teaching by conversation and seminar. True, the stereotype of the German professor was already a figure of fun—the ponderous, humorless, incredibly learned pedant. There were plenty of pedants in the Germany Royce knew; but there were also the finest scholars to be found anywhere; and their technique was not only admirable but imitable. The Americans both admired and imitated it.

To the youthful graduate student, Germany gave more than formal education. The land of the professor was also the land of the lorelei. The thunder of the Teutonic gods was re-echoing in the cataclysmic chords of Wagner. One sailed on the storied Rhine, as had Byron, beneath towering Drachenfels, or followed the steps of Goethe through Cologne Cathedral. There was dueling by the student corps, and the reading of Heine in the coffee shops. There were frauleins to be courted, drinking songs to be sung, steins of beer to be raised in the rathskellers.

The pity is that we know so little of Josiah Royce, countrified product of the American wilderness, as he entered and mingled with the society, at once hoary and revolutionary, exact and Romantic, of the Germany that used to be. By his own testimony he was not a good mixer, so presumably he had to overcome some awkwardness when settling in. But there is no doubt at all about the intellectual thrill that he felt at Leipsic and Göttingen. He could only have had himself in mind when he wrote, in

"Present Ideals of American University Life," concerning the American student privileged to have had the experience of graduate study in Germany: "Lotze or Helmholtz or Mommsen was his master. He could hear and read his fill, in a world of academic industry, and amidst elsewhere unheard of treasuries of books. The air was full of suggestion." [19]

The Germans, having assumed the intellectual hegemony of Europe by 1875, were transforming every field of inquiry with their proverbial thoroughness. They were rethinking logic (Sigwart, Frege), mathematics (Dedekind, Cantor), science (Helmholtz, Mach), psychology (Fechner, Wundt), history (Mommsen, Ranke), classical studies (Wilamowitz, Zeller). The greatest names of the time are still great today. A list of the near-great would be much longer. The spiritual exhilaration of living in a society braced at such a pitch of intellectual effort can be read in the memoirs of those who knew it.

We cannot say exactly how much Josiah Royce assimilated in one year. He has told us about his reading in the Romantic German writers, and he indicates that here began his struggle with the rigors of the new logic. Being, however, a student of philosophy, he is much more explicit about his education in this field: "In Germany I heard Lotze at Göttingen, and was for a while strongly under his influence. The reading of Schopenhauer was another strong influence during my life as a student in Germany. I long paid a great deal of attention to the philosophy of Kant. But during the years before 1890, I never supposed myself to be very strongly under the influence of Hegel. . . ." [20]

Royce was one of those students fortunate enough thus early in life to sit at the feet of a renowned teacher. Hermann Lotze, *the* professor of philosophy of his time, touching with practiced hand the range of philosophical subjects from theology to aesthetics, presided over the mental discipline of pupils who would themselves make an enduring mark in the world: Franz Brentano, Carl Stumpf, and G. E. Müller all became psychologists of the first importance. The foremost metaphysician to come out of Lotze's seminar on philosophy was Josiah Royce.

Students of philosophy flocked to Göttingen from other countries from 1850 to 1880 because Lotze was publishing a series of famous works that gave him an international reputation. His systematic treatise *Mikrokosmus* excited the emulation of other systematizers, while his more limited textbooks on logic, metaphysics, ethics, and psychology did the same for the less ambitious but more scientific.

Lotze's impact on American thought has not yet been adequately estimated. Until recently it was a powerful impact, deciding the course of many an idealist, forcing a reaction by the non-idealists. Borden Parker Bowne, another of Lotze's transatlantic pupils, pillaged the professor's system for elements of a novel version of idealism. John Dewey, at the opposite extreme, recognized in the German thinker a foeman worthy of refutation in *Studies in Logical Theory*. George Santayana, under Royce's direction, and against his own inclinations, was forced to write a dissertation on Lotze.

William James was at once impressed and repelled by Lotze. Admitting a debt in both philosophy and psychology, James adds: "He seems to me the most exquisite of contemporary minds." [21] But James's *Pluralistic Universe* is very severe on Lotze from the standpoint of philosophical thinking. It accuses him of "vicious intellectualism" for treating verbalisms as explanatory principles: "*Call* your a and b distinct, they can't interact; *call* them one, they can." [22] James submitted to Lotze's empirical method, and to what he considered its legitimate results even in abstract thought. He would not submit to the idealistic monism of which he judged Lotze guilty through an illegitimate transfer of attention from examining reality to playing with words.

Royce disagreed with the negative criticism of his German mentor by his Harvard colleague. He took Lotze to be no monist but, as he said to Santayana, "rather Leibnitzian." [23] On this point, Royce is certainly nearer the mark than James. Lotze, an adversary of the absolutism developed in post-Kantian idealism from Fichte to Hegel, was one of the thinkers who helped to undermine Hegelianism in Germany—a consummation that James devoutly wished and enthusiastically applauded while he was lamenting the revival of the Hegelian philosophy in Britain and America.[24]

Royce, on the other hand, demurs at the Lotzean metaphysics where James does not. Lotze's appeal to validity falls under Royce's general indictment of critical rationalism, the confounding of actuality and possibility. And Royce would not admit that Lotze accounts for the place of sentiment in the search for truth. Where Lotze wants the truth for the good of humanity, Royce wants it for its own sake and regardless of its impact on our ideals and aspirations: "Doubt should be earnest." [25] Again, Royce was not so convinced as James about Lotze's empiricism, which he judged inferior to Le Conte's on the score of scientific knowledge.[26]

The Lotzean system was, therefore, not acceptable to Royce, who scarcely refers to it while building his own. His legacy from his Göttingen professor was primarily a matter of spirit, approach, method. Lotze hoped to erect a grand synthesis of human knowledge; so did Royce. Lotze intended to remain hard-headedly empirical without rejecting idealism; so did Royce. Lotze wanted to purify old metaphysics with new logic; so did Royce. Lotze argued for a union of facts and values that would save the uniqueness of each; so did Royce.

Lotze achieved with Royce what is doubtless the highest achievement of any teacher with any pupil: He inspired him to creative reaction rather than to pious imitation. After learning Lotze's system, Royce would never again be moved by Spencer's. After mastering Lotze's technique, Royce would become progressively more dissatisfied with Lotze's system. His mind alerted by Lotze to the dimensions of philosophical problems, he was impelled to look for more satisfactory ways of dealing with them.

His reading at Göttingen gave an undeviating direction to his thoughts. Lotze set him to exploring philosophical literature, and the decisive moment came when graduate student Josiah Royce met the titanic figure of Immanuel Kant. What the *Critique of Pure Reason* means to a young man approaching it for the first time has been eloquently described by Royce in *The Spirit of Modern Philosophy*: "One hears of Kant early in one's life as a student of philosophy. He is said to be hard, perhaps a little dangerous (a thing which of course attracts one hugely!). He is said to be also certainly typical of German speculation, and always worthy of one's efforts if one means to philosophize at all. . . . The *Critique of Pure Reason*, how attractive the name! How wise one will be after criticising the pure reason through the reading of five or six hundred pages of close print!" [27]

Here again, surely, Royce is being autobiographical. Such must have been his mood as he began to read the greatest philosophical masterpiece of the modern world. Kant rolled out for him the map of philosophy with all its twistings, turnings, highways, and blind alleys; and showed him how to find his way by observing such brilliant markers as the subjectivity of space and time, the noumenal world of the thing-in-itself, the authority of reason in the phenomenonal world, the transcendental deduction of the categories, the transcendental unity of apperception.

Royce, as in the case of *Faust,* which he was reading at the same time, never recovered from his original exposure to the *Critique of Pure Reason.* It remained for him the best introduction from which the philosopher might learn to philosophize. He acknowledged with the post-Kantian idealists that, while one could not stop where Kant stopped, one could progress only by marching with the Sage of Königsberg as far as he went, and then advancing beyond him. Royce followed Kant in his systematic thinking until he came to the description of experience: Royce believed that Kant had identified the riddle of riddles, the contribution of the mind to its own knowledge, but that the Kantian analysis of this subjective spontaneity was faulty.

The business of "bringing Kant up to date" (by revising the *Critique of Pure Reason* in the light of the *Critique of Practical Reason* and the *Critique of Judgment*) was a familiar undertaking in the Germany that Royce knew. His own attitude to the undertaking is the subject of his article "Kant's Relation to Modern Philosophic Progress." He pursues the idea in 'Mind and Reality," "The Implications of Self-consciousness," "On Purpose in Thought," and in various lesser items of his bibliography. The Kantian theme runs, more or less diluted, through his books.

The second classical master with whom Royce became acquainted at this time was Arthur Schopenhauer, who had attended Royce's University of Göttingen back in 1809, and who had died within Royce's lifetime (1860). Schopenhauer is another philosopher who appeals to tyros in philosophy, but for rather different reasons than Kant. He is also a thinker who can hold the attention of the mature, as he held Royce.

Schopenhauer is a prose master of an order so high that probably no one will disagree with Royce's opinion that *The World as Will and Idea* is "the most artistic philosophical treatise in existence, if one excepts the best of Plato's *Dia-*

logues."[28] The pessimism of Schopenhauer, an enticing *succès de scandale* to the sophomore, seems a factual report to those with experience of life. The irrationalism of Schopenhauer touches a familiar chord in the minds of more than cynics and existentialists.

Royce considered Schopenhauer an antidote to the shallow optimism which both abhorred, and a philosopher perfectly usable if balanced by equally just ideas on the other side. After reading *The World as Will and Idea,* Royce could not doubt that volition is a cardinal faculty in the apprehension of truth. The author also instructed him in the art of polemical debate: "Schopenhauer is a sort of dealer in deadly weapons. We go to him for a pistol or a knife when our interests are murderous, for he often supplies the most effective means for argumentative success when we want a dialectic victory."[29]

Since Schopenhauer held that *The World as Will and Idea* was the valid outcome of the *Critique of Pure Reason,* Royce had before him a masterly essay in "bringing Kant up to date." This particular attempt he came to regard as unsuccessful; but it was the most acute thing of its kind with which he became familiar during his stay at Leipsic and Göttingen, and his knowledge of what Schopenhauer had made of Kant may have been the most significant acquisition of his German period. When he left for home, he was equipped intellectually to go much farther than he went in a single year of graduate study: He was ready to take the measure of the other post-Kantian idealists, of Fichte, Schelling, and the much more formidable Hegel.

This year of 1875-76 was the decisive one of Royce's intellectual life. It made him a German romanticist in literature, a German idealist in philosophy. He would assimilate fresh ideas of which neither Kant nor Hegel ever heard; but—he himself repeated it time and again—he would never surrender the philosophical insight of his period as a graduate student. He came back from Göttingen an incipient idealist and absolutist. His mission in metaphysics would be to prove, if he could, that all valid philosophical reasoning is both idealistic and absolutistic.

Josiah Royce was a Germanized American thinker.

This explains why one of the tragedies of his life was his survival into the terrible period of World War I. Romantic, scientific, musical Germany became transmogrified before his horrified gaze into a Germany brutal and militant. Only his conception of the contrast can explain the violence of Royce's reaction, the fact that he would not pause to ask whether there might be guilt and innocence on both sides. He viewed the conflict in stark terms of black and white because he felt that the Prussianized Teutons had betrayed more than Western civilization. They had betrayed the Germany of Kant and Goethe, the Germany that Royce loved and believed in. They had betrayed *him*.

He was less fortified against a one-sided interpretation of the struggle because his health was irrevocably gone. His physical and mental debility rendered impossible the judicious appraisal of which he unquestionably would have been capable in his earlier years. No doubt he put his indictment into the terms of his philosophy, picturing the Allies and the Central Powers as, respectively, for and against loyalty. No doubt his object in demanding American intervention was to have his country on the side of those who, in his opinion, were defending the great community. But nowhere do these noble words ring with a more hollow sound than in his propaganda efforts: "The Duties of Americans in the Present War," "The Destruction of the Lusitania," and "The First Anniversary of the Sinking of the Lusitania, May 7th, 1916."

While Bertrand Russell was going to jail for opposing the British war effort, Josiah Royce allowed his moral sense to degenerate into a misguided moralism so perverse that he could castigate the Germans, with astounding rage, as "the wilful and deliberate enemy of the human race," "the enemy of mankind," "these enemies of our country and of mankind." [30] He, who had so clearly seen the mixture of good and evil in the conquest of California, could see in World War I only the hallucinatory image of the good angels versus the bad angels.[31]

Royce's intellectual biography should not be allowed to end in a conclusion so lame and impotent. To his credit, he never capitulated to the fury of the intellectuals who blamed Kant and Hegel for helping to provoke Europe's catastrophe. His "Nietzsche" is an appreciation and not a condemnation. While German thought was being thrust aside, German music silenced, and even the German language avoided as unpatriotic, Royce remained true to the philosophy that he had begun to master at Leipsic and Göttingen. This, too, was loyalty (to what he conceived to be the truth), and it is no reflection on him that his loyalty hastened his death.

III *Harvard*

When Royce returned to the United States in 1876, he went to newly founded Johns Hopkins as one of its first fellows. For two years he pushed his study of philosophy with increasing depth and refinement, and at the end wrote a dissertation on a subject that was to remain a preoccupation with him: "The Possibility of Error."

Meanwhile, he had become familiar with William James. He heard James lecture at Johns Hopkins, and visited him in Cambridge—a beginner come to ask the advice of an old master about what might lie ahead should he adopt philosophy for a career. James gave Royce the encouragement he needed to pursue the vocation, and Royce, who never forgot how he had been heartened at a moment of personal doubt, paid eloquent tribute to his benefactor when he spoke at a gathering in honor of James in 1910.[32]

Royce's first job was not in philosophy. The University of California having offered him a place on the faculty of English literature, he accepted for obvious reasons: He needed to make a living, and California would both return him to his native state and reunite him as a colleague with his old teachers. He joined Sill and Le Conte, lectured to English classes, pursued his research into philosophy, and published his first book: *Primer of Logical Analysis for the Use of Composition Students.*

By now his mind was definitely deflected into the problems of logic, epistemology, and metaphysics, of knowledge and being. He was turning out important papers in which he attacked the task of "bringing Kant up to date." He kept hoping for an appointment at an institution where he might be professionally required to stick to the task. That was one reason for his extensive correspondence with William James, who generously offered to do what he could for his erstwhile pupil on the opposite side of the continent where Royce alone represented technical philosophy.

The other reason for the letters that passed between Cambridge and Berkeley was Royce's anxiety to have his ideas scrutinized by one whose judgment he respected beyond that of anyone else. They discussed the great philosophers. They discussed the worth of the system of Shadworth Hodgson, an English metaphysician of the period. They discussed the articles of Charles Sanders Peirce which were then appearing in the learned journals.

James and Royce read one another's philosophical essays with mutual appreciation. James was struck by Royce's "Schiller's Ethical Studies," "Mind and Reality," and "Kant's Relation to Modern Philosophic Progress." Royce was struck by James's famous article on the meaning and apprehension of space: "The Spatial Quale." James writes to Royce as one who has found his path into philosophy, Royce to James as one still searching for his. It was not yet clear to them, although it is to us, that they were moving in different directions toward contrary philosophies.

The upshot of all this was everything Royce could have hoped for. James got him a temporary appointment to Harvard beginning with the year 1882, and his remarkable ability caused him to be reappointed and added to the permanent staff.

The philosophy faculty of "Royce's" Harvard was one of the most distinguished any university has ever had, and by all odds the finest in the history of higher education in America. It was not a single school of thought, for the members were committed to little more than the proposition that philosophy ought to be studied and taught in an intellectual atmosphere of complete freedom. They not only held variegated metaphysical principles and stood for contrary if not antipathetical systems: They freely criticized one another even in their lectures to the undergraduates.

Royce's thirty-four years in Cambridge saw the assembling of a group of philosophers of whom six members gained a significant place in American thought: William James, George Herbert Palmer, Hugo Münsterberg, George Santayana, Ralph Barton Perry, and, of course, Royce himself.

That James should be the leader of Harvard philosophy was inevitable, he being the leader of American philosophy, and a leader of world philosophy. He made pragmatism famous as the American style. He did not invent the method of looking for "what works" (Peirce did), but he expounded the method in forceful prose that caught the attention of intellectuals in

Europe and America. He knew or corresponded with practically all the prominent philosophers of his time from Herbert Spencer to Henri Bergson. He put into the market place of ideas two masterpieces on their respective subjects: *Principles of Psychology* and *The Varieties of Religious Experience.* His reputation was that of the most brilliant anti-Hegelian of the Western world, the resolute champion of pluralism and radical empiricism against monism and rationalism.

The independence of Harvard in choosing professors is proven by the fact that Palmer resided on the same faculty with James. Palmer stood for that which James disliked most. He was a follower of Hegel, and a follower devoid of the ability to do more with Hegelian thought than to dilute it with superficial optimism and fashionable religion. James often mentions Palmer as a thinker whose thought constituted an impediment to genuine philosophizing.

Münsterberg was a psychologist who came to Harvard from Germany at James's behest to take charge of the psychological laboratory, but again there was no question of discipleship. Münsterberg held, and stated that he held, important reservations about the ideas and theories defended by James in *Principles of Psychology;* and he would not accept James's handling of religious experience in the *Varieties.* Their differences may have prompted rather than hampered James (who preferred bold opposition to servile imitation) in his decision to bring Münsterberg to Harvard.

Then there were the two bright young men of the philosophy department. The greater of the two was Santayana, Royce's pupil and compelled by Royce to write the dissertation on Lotze. Santayana successfully resisted the appeal of Royce's system as he had resisted Lotze's, dropped idealism without shifting to pragmatism, and over the subsequent years erected a system of his own—a sophisticated form of what he chose to call "materialism."

Excepting Palmer, the least important of the important Harvard philosophers was Perry. He came to a version of realism that put him in the camp of the New Realists; but he probably is more significant today because of the criticism he directed at Royce's interpretation of realism and because of his writings on James.

With such a staff, Harvard attracted undergraduates who elected to study philosophy. This suited Royce. He was a natural pedagogue, one who delighted in prompting youthful minds to the inquiries that had begun to pique his own intellect when he was at their level. The testimony of his pupils to his ability to simplify technical philosophy can be corroborated by his writings, especially by *The Spirit of Modern Philosophy,* than which there is no more lucid, entertaining, and accurate presentation of the German idealistic systems from Kant to Schopenhauer.

The official work done by Royce at Harvard was prodigious. He taught classes in almost every department of philosophical study: logic, metaphysics, psychology, natural theology, the philosophy of science, the history of philosophy.[33] To most of them he brought a fresh rigor and virility, and for hundreds of beginners philosophy first became a live subject as they listened to Royce. Concerned for the quality of education in America when James and Dewey were discussing what to do about it, Royce wrote articles like "Present Ideals of American University Life," "The Freedom of Teaching," and "Is there a Science of Education?"

While he was learning to simplify his ideas for his students, Royce was learning to sharpen them for the professionals. His thought matured, his system was built, his great books were written. Harvard gave him opportunity and scope for his thinking. It provided practical evidence for one of his guiding philosophical concepts. Reminiscing, he remarked: "The best concrete instance of the life of a community with which I have had the privilege to become well acquainted has been furnished to me by my own Seminary. . . ."[34]

In spite of the pleasure of being at Harvard, Royce was not willing to compromise his integrity to ensure his place there. He might have jeopardized his future and he did lose a thousand dollars, when, before his professorship and with a wife and family to support, he refused to deliver the Lowell Lectures. It was a great honor that President Charles Eliot should make the offer to so recent an addition to the university staff; and Royce was not unmindful of the honor or the stipend or the chance to expound his philosophical ideas before a notable gathering of scholars. The material for the Lowell Lectures lay to hand in his voluminous notes.

But the lectureship carried a condition. The lecturer was expected to sign a brief statement of belief. Upon being informed of the condition, Royce declined both it and the lectureship. Perhaps, given his distaste for formalism in religious creeds, he would have acted thus even had he believed the one presented to him. More likely, his thoughts about theology still being fluid, he could not honestly affix his signature to it. So he lost the Lowell Lectures—and the audience lost the ablest man available for the appointment. Royce took his assembled data and put them into the first of his major works, the volume that established him as a thinker to be watched by his fellow philosophers: *The Religious Aspect of Philosophy.*[35]

Royce's integrity was such that he desired only the most demanding scrutiny of his publications, while he took it as tacitly agreed that he would not restrain himself when paying his adversaries the same compliment. Harvard, as a result, saw some magnificent philosophical disputation within the philosophy faculty. Integrity in this sense, however, is not always enough; and in criticizing one particular opponent Royce went entirely too far. As he had been unfair with John Charles Frémont in history, so did he now become unfair with Francis Ellingwood Abbot in philosophy.

The Abbot affair originated in the Harvard principle of having different philosophies expounded from the same chair. When Royce left on his Australian tour in 1888, he was replaced by Abbot, who delivered a series of lectures and then published them under the title *The Way out of Agnosticism.* Abbot's metaphysics contrasted with what Royce had been telling the same classes in that it purported to establish pantheism by basing itself on the methods of science. The heart of Abbot's system was what he termed the "American Theory of Universals," defined thus: "To the American theory, the sole object of knowledge is *the Universal Kind and the Individual Thing as necessarily correlated in the real genus-in-itself.*"[36]

Royce reviewed Abbot's book for the *International Journal of Ethics,* of which he was an editor. He could not have approached the task in a very impartial frame of mind since he already held a low opinion of Abbot, whom he had pummeled in a prior review of Abbot's *Scientific Theism.* He had pictured Abbot as a weak echo of the traditional objective idealists; had derided his argument as "arrant scholasticism," "unphilosophical and antiquated"; and had jibed at him for having "a not uncommon but highly amusing state of mind." [37]

The animus of "Abbot's Scientific Theism" was good-humor itself beside that of "Dr. Abbot's 'Way out of Agnosticism'." The "American Theory of Universals" is pronounced to be nothing more revolutionary than Hegel's concrete universal misunderstood: "Dr. Abbot's doctrine is so far 'American' as it is Hegel with the subtlety of that crafty old fox left out." [38] Royce expends fifteen pages on an unrelenting, hostile, philosophical analysis, but on more than that: He as good as states that he wants to ruin Abbot's reputation in philosophy. Abbot appears as a man of "more courage than sense of humor," afflicted with "an especially keen hatred for sceptically critical reflection upon fundamental truths," and therefore liable to mislead "immature or imperfectly trained minds." [39]

> The agnostic, meanwhile, who should actually be led "out" by Dr. Abbot, would be of necessity a person of so unreflective a mind, so ignorant of the history of thought, so badly afraid of italics, so little grounded in his agnosticism, that, whatever humanity might dictate as to the value of any pious effort to benefit his soul, there may be grave doubts whether his philosophically self-critical powers were worth the trouble of saving.[40]

It is unlikely that any scholar would have let so scathing a review pass without protest. Francis Ellingwood Abbot, vain, sensitive, and bellicose, did not confine himself to protesting. He tried to gain redress through a savage retort offered to the *International Journal of Ethics,* and then, believing that he was being deliberately balked by the machinations of Royce, he dashed off two pamphlets in which he appealed to Harvard to censure its professor for conduct unbecoming a member of the faculty.

> It is not "fair criticism"; it is not "criticism" at all; and I do not hesitate to characterize it deliberately as a disgrace to Harvard University and to American scholarship. . . . Most of all, I deny Dr. Royce's self-assumed right to club every philosopher whose reasoning he can neither refute nor understand.[41]

> The essence of the fraud lay in *ostentatiously and publicly using Harvard's name to obtain credit for a false and malicious libel,*

and thereby falsifying the certificate of good moral character conferred on him through Harvard's official appointment.[42]

The university committee refused to act in the matter, ruling judicially that Royce wrote his review not as a Harvard professor but as a professional student of philosophy, so that his "professional warning" to Abbot's readers could not be construed as falling within the committee's jurisdiction. The rebuff sent Abbot furiously to Webster's Dictionary, where he found himself triumphantly vindicated by the synonym "professional" attached to the word "professorial." He also found other adjectives applicable to Royce—mean, vulgar, cowardly, violent, Boeotian.

Then Abbot bethought himself that perhaps Royce was simply embarrassed about the terms of an apology, and so he decided to help him out. Abbot had printed a form on which were listed his indispensable conditions for peace—retraction of the charges that he was pretentious and that he borrowed from Hegel, and also of the professional warning that his ability in philosophy was not up to the demands he made on it. This card he mailed to Royce along with a note stating that the only thing required was Royce's signature on the dotted line. Royce, for some reason, and to Abbot's amazement, returned the card unsigned. The controversy petered out amid a cloud of Abbot's colorful rhetoric.

Meanwhile it had moved from the academic halls into the public domain. It was argued through four issues of *The Nation*. Abbot and Royce's lawyer, Joseph Warner, discussed the question of just who was libeling whom, with Warner doing his best to placate an implacable adversary, with Abbot marveling at the iniquity of those arrayed against him. Two greater names chimed in on opposite sides of the Royce-Abbot dispute, Charles Sanders Peirce and William James.

Pierce. I believe that the prevalent opinion among competent men would be that Prof. Royce's warning is an unwarranted aspersion. . . . How far a spirit of rivalry may have influenced him no man can say, Prof. Royce least of all . . . It was a brutal life-and-death struggle from the first. . . . Dr. Abbot, on the other hand, stood like a baited bull, bewildered at such seemingly motiveless hostilities.[43]

James. Reviews of philosophical books in technical journals

> are apt to be destructive—that is what philosophers expect of one another. . . . Mr. Abbot's remedy of heaping personal outrages upon Prof. Royce and his motives admits of no excuse but a pathological one.[44]

The truth is that Royce and Abbot were both guilty—Royce more than Abbot because he started the personal animadversions, Abbot more than Royce because he turned brutally insulting. At this distance, the thing looks like a comedy rather than a *cause celèbre,* and it could be termed such except for the sad spectacle of Royce falling so far below his customary standards of philosophical debate.

He adhered scrupulously to his standards when debating with his leading intellectual adversary. Royce and James remained good friends personally and stubborn antagonists philosophically during their twenty-eight years together at Harvard, and this despite the fact that their exchanges were neither tepid nor deferential. Perry recalls,

> In 1903-1904 James gave a metaphysical seminary in which he defended pluralism against monistic idealism. On a certain occasion, when he had intended to criticize Royce, he was ill and had Royce fill his place. The latter, quite equal to the occasion, went to the class armed with James's copy of his *World and the Individual,* from which he read aloud some of James's most spirited marginal notes, such as "what an ass of a realist," interjected opposite a passage in which Royce had written, "Our realist . . . may hereupon say, etc." If Royce proceeded further he read, "I cannot imagine what is gained by Royce's vague and floundering account"—"Bah! What silly quibbling"—"Blind and confused."[45]

Royce, who knew how to put impish humor even into metaphysical discourse, must have held a slightly uproarious class that day. Not that he would have ridiculed James; but his enormous respect for the great pragmatist never deterred him from making the retort satirical when he felt satire to be appropriate. Their continuing joust was not carried on with blunted spears or wooden swords.

They were able to come to grips with one another because of the extent to which they agreed. Both were practical, empirical, and averse to wayward romantic philosophizing. Both were voluntarists who allotted a commanding function to the will in the formation of rational judgments. The point at issue between them was the metaphysical system that best accounted for the practical, the empirical, and the voluntaristic. Their differences could not be resolved because, while Royce remained an absolute idealist of the post-Kantian type, James was trying to disintegrate both absolutism and idealism with the solvent of pragmatism.

James the pluralist includes Royce among the believers in "The Mad Absolute," to use the title of his note on the subject.[46] He recoiled from the theory with so much vehemence on the ground that it stifled human freedom by absorbing individuals into an all-encompassing being, with no independent action left to them. Epistemologically, he considered the theory superfluous since the orientation of ideas toward objects could be explained without it: "Royce makes the Absolute do the aiming and intending. I make the chain of empirical intermediaries do it." [47]

If absolutism is so obviously hopeless, why are so many thinkers persuaded by it? James argues—"vicious intellectualism" of the Lotze variety, the recourse to verbalisms such that one's arbitrary definitions dictate the character of objective reality. He thought Royce only too apt a pupil of Lotze.[48] The upshot was his verdict on Royce's philosophizing: "There isn't a tight joint in his system; not one." [49]

Royce might have said the same thing about James, for he found pragmatism intellectually anarchic until it had been caught up in the only philosophy that rendered it rational—absolute idealism.

"Ideas," says Royce in *The World and the Individual,* "ideas are like tools. They are there for an end." [50] He believed like any Jamesean pragmatist in practical results as the criterion of truth. He was as interested as James in "cash value" and "what works." But Royce's interpretation of these phrases could not be the same if only because he discovered what he took to be a sounder interpretation in another pragmatist, the original pragmatist, Charles Sanders Peirce. James gave to the individual the right to verify truth from his personal experience. Peirce opposed this criterion and declared that "Truth is public." [51] Royce agreed with Peirce (who notoriously parted company with James, dropped the term "pragmatist," and coined for himself the neologism "pragmaticist").

By accepting so much of pragmatism, Royce felt that he could find James guilty of self-contradiction, of in fact and by necessity going beyond the individual to the larger general consensus, on pain of confounding private delusion with objective truth. Royce's article "The Eternal and the Practical" points out that there is not, and cannot be, a pure pragmatist who comprehends his pragmatism, since his criterion of truth implicitly reaches out toward wider and wider circles of verification.

> Hence, at the moment of expressing one's pragmatism, one loves to appeal to well recognized objective truths—to evolution, to common sense, to whatever is likely to seem universally valid.[52]
>
> . . . .
>
> As a teacher, then, the pragmatist is much like another professor. He has his little horde of maxims; he proclaims the truth; he refutes errors; he asserts that we ought to believe thus and so; and thus lays down the law as vigorously as do other men."[53]

James was no more convinced by Royce than Royce by James. They crossed swords in print, in lecture halls, at their front gates. They attacked and counterattacked; they stated premises and inferred conclusions; they made distinctions that sometimes made a difference and sometimes did not. In short, they engaged in philosophical disputation.

They ended farther apart than when they had started. Doubtless it was inevitable. Disagreement is not unknown in philosophy, and if Aristotle could not agree with Plato, or Schopenhauer with Hegel, there is no reason to be surprised that Royce could not agree with James. They were self-proclaimed voluntarists, and there is no small element of the will in their philosophizing.

The James-Royce antithesis must be reckoned one of the major themes of American philosophy. The commentators have discussed it and will continue to discuss it, not merely in academic terms: On each side there is what phrase-maker William James called a "living option"—a type of philosophizing that still challenges assent.[54] James and Royce challenge contemporary thinkers, as they challenged one another, to assent—or to do some very hard thinking in order to win the right to dissent.

They were implacable dissenters, each to the other, because they held in common the principle that truth is to be preferred above friendship. More accurately, they regarded the working out of their conflicting philosophies face-to-face as one of the strongest bonds of their mutual affection. Neither could live in an ivory tower. Each felt the need of reasoned disagreement where agreement was impossible. Each valued the other as a whetstone of the finest kind on which to sharpen the edge of his metaphysical wit—as the embodiment par excellence of the most formidable opposition, so that victory here, if it could be attained, would be a permanent gain not to be compromised by lesser men. Royce and James had good reason to thank the good fortune that brought them together so closely for so long.

It is a rare intellectual experience to follow their developing dialectic through the material presented by Ralph Barton Perry in *The Thought and Character of William James*. One of the best introductions to either philosopher is the stages in his criticism of his friendly enemy. This is especially true of James on Royce, for the pragmatist felt that absolutism was morally objectionable long before he could see any insuperable rational case against it. Royce posed the absolutist arguments so powerfully that James, in sheer intellectual honesty, had no alternative: He saw that he must settle down to a mastery of the arguments, and then, depending on his final verdict, either champion them as true or assail them as false. The process by which he became their assailant spans the interval between his judgments on two of Royce's books: *The Religious Aspect of Philosophy* (1885) and *The World and the Individual* (1899). The first he admired. The second he deplored; and he remained thenceforth uncompromisingly anti-absolutist, anti-Royce.[55]

Royce did not go through any such progression with regard to pragmatism. Having arrived at Harvard with his mind made up, his rejection of James from the start was inevitable. Royce accumulates anti-pragmatist polemics and stocks his arsenal of thought with them. He becomes with maturity more willing to speak candidly to his older colleague. There is never, at any time, any fear in his mind that, after all, James just might be right about pragmatism.

The word "manly" is one that appears frequently in the writings of both James and Royce, for both of whom it was among the highest commendations of any thinker. Taken in the sense of courage combined with chivalry, each could properly apply the epithet to the other, for they were equally manly in spirit and attitude. Never ill-tempered with one another, they never wrangled. One of the pleasanter sides to their relationship is the way they could joke about each other. Royce titillated his class with James's gloss on *The World and the Individual.* James wrote to Royce: "The Absolute himself must get great fun out of being you." [56] James had only the warmest regard for Royce, even when denouncing him for a misguided absolutist. Royce would not let his aversion for pragmatism mar his admiration of James. His utterances over three decades prove that he was not simply honoring the precept *de mortuis nil nisi bonum* when, after James's death in 1910, he wrote the appreciative memoir "William James and the Philosophy of Life." [57]

They were masterful personalities and acute thinkers, these two professors who enlivened Harvard at the turn of the century. America has not had another duumvirate of philosophers comparable to William James and Josiah Royce.

CHAPTER 3

Royce's Approach to Philosophy

JOSIAH ROYCE was one of the boldest and one of the most cautious of modern philosophers. No metaphysical abstraction, no theorem of advanced mathematical logic, no flight of the imagination into the higher reaches of speculation, whether scientific or theological, was too daring for him to follow. No practical experience was too crude for him to inspect. His paraphrase of Terence, inserted into a different context, expresses perfectly his attitude toward life, thought, and experience: "I regard nothing real as *a me alienum*."[1] He was willing to assimilate truth and being wherever he found them, and it was not his habit to restrict his search so that he might avoid being intellectually embarrassed by facts with which his philosophy could not cope. Rather, he found with Hegelian intensity a virile joy in the intellectual subjugation of the most resistant elements of an apparently intractable cosmos.

So grandiose an aspiration suggests the hubris upon which nemesis follows: In philosophical terms, that philosopher is generally the first to fail who cannot recognize his own limitations and tries to do too much. Royce was familiar with this axiom. He saw it demonstrated in practice by Spencer, Mill, and Lotze, all three of whom became increasingly ineffectual during his lifetime. The stumblings of the great post-Kantians he both followed as a student and explained as a professor. He was not minded to repeat the experience of those who threw away the compass while sailing the metaphysical ocean, voyaged onward into the unknown, and proclaimed themselves masters of their fate when they were in fact lost in a trackless waste.

Royce is circumspect enough to maintain his bearings from point-to-point. His compass may appear defective; he may occasionally misread it; but his steady determination is to keep himself from being pulled off course by his desires or his instincts. He has learned from the logicians and the scientists. His thought is complex, but not chaotic. Illogical at times, he is hardly ever subjective, irrational, or mystical. If it is possible, and even mandatory, to disagree with him, it is never fair criticism to call him unintelligible.

The consistency of his systematic philosophy through its long development has been questioned. That there are distinct stages in it is as evident to us as it was to him, but, despite the lush profusion of philosophical theories to which he resorts, his contention about unity pervading his mental biography has not been refuted. From beginning to end, he is unmistakably an absolute idealist. His arguments vary; his philosophy does not.[2]

I *Philosophy in Perspective*

Royce's idealism is noteworthy for its relation to the classical systems of the past. Where James constructed his pragmatism by placing less reliance on old modes of thought and more on present experience, Royce found that most of his thinking had already been done for him. Indeed, he tended to suspect any philosopher who claimed to be startlingly original. When he looked back over the history of philosophy from the Greeks to his contemporaries, he could not believe that it was largely a mass of sophisticated error, a succession of gratuitously grounded systems that cancel one another and must be by-passed because they are no longer relevant. His purpose was to isolate and to use the truths and insights in them, even in those most hostile to idealism.

He treated the dead as he treated the living: He made them become, willy nilly, witnesses to the correctness of his system. That is why he was no mere chronicler, but rather an inveterate pursuer of living ideas handed down to him for incorporation into his own thought. He was not interested in what he could not use. He was interested in "the spirit of modern philosophy"—the line of traditional philosophizing that he considered an accumulating treasure of sound, mutually enlightening ideas.

Not so drastic as Hegel in claiming that previous philosophy was but a propaedeutic to his own, Royce considered his thought in its essentials to be the justifiable outcome of what had gone before. He was no eclectic sorting out bits and pieces of various philosophies in order to prove that the philosophers could be made consistent with one another. He *was* a true believer in the principle that past thought, insofar as it has any worth, is never merely past but rather carries definite contributions to the present. "Faithfulness to history," he says, "is the beginning of creative wisdom." [3]

By "history" he means almost explicitly Kant and post-Kantianism. That he was well versed in the broad development of Western philosophy is shown by his articles in Baldwin's *Dictionary of Philosophy and Psychology*—articles on the terminology of the Greeks, the Scholastics, Kant, and Hegel. In the corpus of his works he refers knowledgeably to Plato and Aristotle, to Augustine and Aquinas, to Descartes and Spinoza, to Locke and Hume. Berkeley provides him with the one notion fundamental to idealism, the notion, namely, that only ideas are knowable. Yet all of the rest are, in his treatment of the subject, background material for Kant-and-after.

The "spirit" of *The Spirit of Modern Philosophy* is that of Kant, Fichte, Schelling, Hegel, and Schopenhauer. The *Lectures on Modern Idealism* are lectures on these masters. Royce views the great systems from the standpoint of his important early article: "Kant's Relation to Modern Philosophic Progress." His effort is always to survey the foundations laid by the creator of the tradition, to decide how far others had built well on the foundations, and to advance the construction with some new architecture.

Kant performed the service of asking the questions that subsequent philosophers would have to answer. This being Royce's opinion, Kant is for him the real starting-point, or at least turning-point, in the history of philosophy.

> After all, the spiritual world that Kant bade us build is the modern world; and Kant is the true hero of all modern thought. If in one sense it is only by transcending him and even by forgetting some of his limitations that we are to triumph, he is none the less forever our guide. Kant is, if you like, the homely and somewhat incongruous figure, a sort of John Brown of our century of speculative warfare. Derided as a rebel and an enemy of the faith by many of his own time, he dies before the modern

> conflict is fairly begun, but his soul goes marching on through the whole of it.[4]

Royce, with the understood reservations, accepts the claim inherent in Kant's title: *Prolegomena to Every Future Metaphysic;* and he looks at reality first from the perspective of the *Critique of Pure Reason* and the *Critique of Practical Reason.* The dominant issues of modern philosophy are posed for him by the transcendental deduction of the categories and the transcendental unity of apperception—the attempt of the critical philosophy to state the conditions of knowledge of the self.

Kant made Royce an empiricist, but an empiricist with a difference. The *Critique of Pure Reason* states that all knowledge begins with experience since "thoughts without content are empty." This is not the crude empiricism of Locke, who likens the mind to a blank sheet on which facts leave an imprint like a seal on wax. Kant adds that the mind impresses forms on the matter it receives through the senses—the forms of space, time, and the categories—and what follows is the Kantian distinction between things-in-themselves and the things we know; between the world of noumena, which is real, and the world of phenomena, which is a function of knowledge.

Experience, empirical fact, rules the phenomenal world. Kant formulates this part of his philosophy in a sententious assertion that Royce quotes and requotes with approval: *Nur in der Erfahrung ist Wahrheit*—"Truth is only in experience." It being obvious that no individual actually perceives everything he knows, Kant breaks experience down into two parts: first, what *is* perceived directly; second, what Royce calls "conceptual constructions" (borrowing the term from Karl Pearson). These latter are the background of immediacy. They are empirical facts even though out of sight. According to Royce:

> If you ask what truth these conceptual constructions possess, your answer must at any moment be: They possess a truth which I at least do not observe or find as a fact of my experience. And yet, without doubt, you are disposed to view all these facts as of the nature of empirical facts. When is experience not experience? The answer is: When its facts are what most of your acknowledged facts of the realm of experience nearly always are, namely, conceptual constructions.[5]

This is where Royce begins to "bring Kant up to date." The need for an analysis of what lies beyond the moment is the premise of "Kant's Relation to Modern Philosophic Progress." The conclusion is that a better analysis than the Kantian is demanded. Royce's analysis results in the three types of conceptual construction that seem to him to make sense of experience: "Acknowledgment of the Past," "Anticipation of the Future," and "Acknowledgment of a Universe of Truth." [6] He thinks that these three allow us to get rid of Kant's elaborate apparatus of the categories. Spontaneity, the activity of the mind in the knowing process, is retained; but the nature of its contribution to knowledge is revised.

Kant's critical philosophy gives to the mind the function of constructing a knowable universe. If the content has to come from outside the mind, the content is nothing to us until it has been rendered intelligible to us. We cannot say what laws the things-in-themselves obey; but we know that the things of experience must conform to the laws of the reason, or they could not enter the reason. To become intelligible, they must submit to the subjective conditions of intelligibility. We are sure of our knowledge in a field like geometry because geometry reflects the laws of space, and space is subjective. Royce follows the Kantian argument to the summation: "If our thought, as a process of comprehending our experience, is obliged to treat the facts before it as conforming to rational laws, in order to think them at all, well, then, the facts of experience, being once for all facts of inner life, will have to conform to law, and that will be the end of it." [7]

Royce, too, believed in the legislative character of the mind in the apprehension of truth: "Change the fashions of our mental activity, and nobody can tell how radically you would change our whole conception of the universe." [8] He gave the idea a non-Kantian turn, after he had read the post-Kantians, by abandoning the things-in-themselves and putting rational intelligibility into the noumenal as well as the phenomenal world. Kant rules out metaphysics. Royce is a metaphysician par excellence.

So far Royce has shown Kant dealing with the individual knower who subjects experience to the laws of his own personal rationality. It is *you* and *I severally* who put laws into our respective worlds, for our minds do not interact. Yet we end up in the same world, along with other sentient beings who possess the same constructive powers, so that there rises the fundamental problem of how this interrelationship can be accounted for on Kantian terms. How is community of experience possible?

It is possible, according to Kant, only because the individual looks beyond his limited experience and conceives it as if it were unlimited, as if his finite mind were capable of observing all the facts that can be observed by anyone, and of knowing all conceptual constructions immediately. There is a *virtual* self to which we all implicitly appeal, and which brings us together in a universe that we can understand and investigate together. This self is ideal rather than real, but nonetheless explanatory in the critical philosophy, being a condition of the common knowledge that we manifestly possess. Royce's phraseology is that each of us tries to think like "the ideal man." [9]

Royce was not satisfied with Kant's virtual self, which he thought had to be real if it were to be really explanatory. There is, nonetheless, a clear resemblance between Kant and Royce when the latter argues that the removal of the finite conditions of our knowledge would permit us a direct insight into absolute experience: "The difference is merely one of span." [10] This statement goes right to the center of the Roycean system of philosophy. Royce is forever trying to improve on Kant with a more plausible account of our conceptual constructions—of the element we add to the given of the moment. Time, therefore, becomes of great concern to him; for "Acknowledgment of the Past," like "Anticipation of the Future," is a conceptual construction that combines with the present in a single experience.

> To sum up, from this point of view the end of thought appears to be: That experience past and future should be conceived as one whole with a necessary connection of parts; that the present and immediately given content of consciousness should be found to be, not alone significant nor enough, but a moment in a world of life; that the relations conceived as necessary for one part of the time-stream should be conceived as necessary for the whole time-stream. And the end of thought is realized in the act of constructing the image of possible experience. For by experience we mean, in addition to what is given, that which is conceived as past and future.[11]

The agreement of Royce with Kant, great on the theoretical level, is even greater on the level of ethics, politics, and religion. The *Critique of Practical Reason* deals with the autonomy of the will, freedom, the categorical imperative, and the kingdom of ends. All of these, however redefined, reappear in Royce.

For Kant, the idea of duty is of supreme importance because it alone touches the noumenal world. The self discovered by introspective psychology is only a phenomenon, a transcendental object conditioned by the subjective forms of the mind. The self as a moral agent is a thing-in-itself. The categorical imperative, going beyond experience, lays down a universal law that duty is to be done for the sake of duty, and such that the act of the individual may be a model for all humanity. It implies that the will is free. It implies that God exists.

The critical philosophy, therefore, describes two worlds in which we live—the noumenal and the phenomenal, the free and the determined, the moral and the scientific. The extent to which Royce follows Kant is striking. Even the language is often much the same. Kant's "duty for duty's sake" is not unlike Royce's "loyalty to loyalty"; his "kingdom of ends" is not unlike Royce's "community of interpretation"; and this categorical imperative from Roycean ethics could be from the *Critique of Practical Reason*: "Therefore the rule of conduct is: Act as thou wouldst wish to have acted were all the consequences of thy act, for all the world of being, here and now given as a fact of thine own present consciousness." [12]

To read Royce on Kant is to get an impression of an admiring commentator surveying a mastermind without any illusions about the times when the master goes profoundly astray. This is precisely the attitude of the post-Kantian idealists. Royce notes the reason for the discrepancy: "Kant had a very singular power of holding his judgment suspended regarding matters that almost any disciple of Kant is at once tempted to decide, and to decide in a way that leads to a modification of the Kantian doctrines." [13]

This process had begun in Kant's time; it continued into Royce's. The great names are Fichte, Schelling, Hegel, Schopenhauer.

It is a paradox and a truism of the history of philosophy that while Kant intended to expose metaphysics as an illusory attempt to know the noumenal world through subjective forms that apply only to phenomena, yet the very arguments of the *Critique of Pure Reason* led almost immediately to an efflorescence of speculative metaphysics on a scale unmatched since the high Middle Ages. Royce has shown why. The thinkers who followed the guide-lines laid down in Konigsberg felt that Kant himself had set up paper barriers between them and their destination. They began to join what he had left asunder. They dropped overboard the *ding-an-sich,* the thing-in-itself, the unknowable Kant-knew-not-what that was supposed to supply the content cast into rational form by the apparatus of space, time, and the categories. They redefined the Kantian self to mean that there is a universal self that is not only virtual but real. They made of this universal self the root principle of thought and being. They began to map and chart a version of reality that became more astonishing as they proceeded, and would certainly have astonished Kant, whose authority was being invoked as the father of it all. (When he was introduced to post-Kantianism by Fichte, he promptly disowned it.)

Six years before Kant's death a young professor of philosophy named Hegel proposed an ambitious program to "bring Kant up to date." Royce puts the Hegelian proposal into the nutshell of a single sentence: "From the Kantian philosophy, he says, a great, new creative movement is to grow, and the central idea of this new movement will be the doctrine of the absolute and infinite self, whose constructive processes shall explain the fundamental laws of the world." [14]

Royce was fascinated by the way the Hegelian program was worked out in Germany. He followed in minute detail the succession of systems from Fichte's subjective idealism through Schelling's objective idealism and Hegel's absolute idealism to Schopenhauer's voluntaristic idealism. He plunders the masterworks for principles and theories: *The Vocation of Man* (Fichte), *The System of Transcendental Idealism* (Schelling), *The Phenomenology of Mind* (Hegel), *The World as Will and Idea* (Schopenhauer). Without these volumes, Royce's philosophy could not have been what it was.

Fichte was the first in the field with a revision of the critical philosophy based on a new transcendental deduction of the categories, and a new explanation of the transcendental unity of apperception. He brings together the various elements that are separated in Kant by attributing everything to the self, which determines the content as well as the form of knowledge. Fichte's true self is Kant's virtual self become real, the universal absolute self that knows all truth and has all experience because it makes both. The emphasis is on activity, on the effort of the will, rather than on the abstract intellect; and the problem for Fichte is to find out why the true self should indulge in universe building. This train of thought leads to a system of ethical idealism in which objective reality exists to give us the opportunity to act in conformity with the moral law. Fichte unites the theoretical reason and the practical reason of Kant.

> The meaning is that the world is the material for my duty, made manifest in my experience. Fortune, limitations, individual selfhood, social life, freedom, immortality—these are incidents in the endless undertaking. Experience seems foreign, just in order that our duty may be done in acts that win control over experience. Such, in the briefest outline, is Fichte's result.[15]

> Thus, then, each of us builds his own world. He builds it in part unconsciously; and therefore he seems to his ordinary thought not to have built it at all, but merely to find it.[16]

Fichtean thoughts like these made Royce an ethical idealist. The whole treatment of the "theoretical ought" in *The World and the Individual* comes out of Fichte, out of the theory that facts are acknowledged by the individual so that he may have something to *do,* which in turn means that there is a teleology that directs everything toward an *end.* Speaking for himself, Royce says: "The Category of the Ought may thus be defined as implying three subordinate Categories; first, that of the Objectivity of all particular facts; secondly, that of the Subjectivity of the grounds for our acknowledgment of every particular fact; thirdly, that of the universal Teleology which, from our point of view, constitutes the essence of all facts." [17]

"Mind and Reality" describes the theory of the theoretical "ought" more succinctly: "The certainty of an external world is the fixed determination to make one, now and henceforth." [18]

Royce learned from Fichte something besides technical metaphysics. He learned a philosophical mood. For both philosophers, speculation about the world and its meaning is not just idle abstraction, or the sober suggestion of technical answers to technical questions. It is a way of life in the Socratic sense, a "vocation" to use Fichte's term. It would be fair to say of Royce what he says of Fichte, that "in all his lengthy and frequently very technical writings, he after all never merely argues: he appeals to more than your understanding; he appeals to your honor, to your dignity of soul, to agree with his system." [19]

Moving on to Schelling, Royce discovered what was wrong with Fichte—he was too subjective. Schelling rejects the notion that facts can be reasoned out in Fichtean fashion, and to right the balance he adds to the word "idealism" the word "objective." The Absolute now appears in the guise, not of a moralist, but of an artist. The external world is now to be explained through *Naturphilosophie*, or the interpretation of scientific data in terms of idealism.

Naturphilosophie has often been mocked for its cosmic speculations, and Royce agrees that Schelling did not have his feet as firmly on the ground as he thought: "His fault lay in his self-assurance, in his impatience, and in his determination to tell nature at once upon meeting her precisely what she meant." [20] At the same time, Royce traces three genuine scientific ideas back to Schelling: The ideas of the unity of science, of evolutionary development, and of the importance of energy as a physical hypothesis. Royce considers this part of *Naturphilosophie* a bridge between post-Kantian thought and the remarkable growth of science in the nineteenth century, for "by thus reshaping the old ideas into modern forms, it prepared them to become leading ideas for a later generation of serious scientific workers." [21] The trouble with Schelling is that he surrounds his valid insights with too much wayward Romanticism.

Hegel is for Royce, as we have seen, the philosopher who understood the "logic of passion," and whose *Phenomenology of Mind* remains the premier philosophical document of the Romantic movement. The Hegelian system of absolute idealism, springing from Kant and influenced by Fichte and Schelling, purports to explain finite things as momentary expressions of infinite reason: "Whatever is real is rational." But the Hegelian universe moves through time according to the dialectic of thesis, antithesis, and synthesis, so that among its salient characteristics are the apparent irrationalities of conflict, error, and evil itself.

Hence Royce's refusal to accept the common view of Hegel as an extravagant rationalist: "Spirituality lives by self-differentiation into mutually opposing forces, and by victory in and over these oppositions. This law it is that Hegel singles out and makes the basis of his system. This is the logic of passion which he so skillfully diagnoses, and so untiringly and even mercilessly applies to all life." [22]

The problem of evil is solved by defining virtue as the triumph over its opposite: No evil, no opportunity for virtue. The virtuous man becomes so by struggling with the vices to which he is tempted and by standing with head erect amid the tragedies and buffooneries of life. On this point Royce frankly confesses to being an Hegelian: "All this I set down here, not merely because I believe it, although indeed I do. . . ." [23]

There are many other common points between the two thinkers. Hegel's concrete universal (the nub of Royce's controversy with Abbot), by which all reality is declared to be an organism wherein individuals gain their being and their meaning—this concrete universal rules Royce's world of appreciation or value, as distinct from the world of factual description, for "the community of truth, in the world of such spirits, would be rather of the Hegelian type of universality, than of the ordinary type of the more abstract universality." [24]

Again, Royce's quest for a theory of the community took a decisive direction after he read Hegel. The common elements are patent: The state as a larger self, the state as the creator of human personality, the state as the march of God through the world.

Still, Royce refused to be labeled a Hegelian because he had too many qualifications to insist on. He recoiled in particular from the Hegelian cosmology, "Hegel's most unfinished and weakest undertaking." [25] Hegel was, like Fichte and Schelling, too inclined to offer grandiose scientific theories without scientific evidence.

This is where Schopenhauer becomes important. The vessel of a monumental animosity toward Hegel and Hegelian absolutism, Schopenhauer grimly pursues irrationalities that he considers beyond rational explanations. Royce pictures him as the thinker who broke out of the hothouse of post-Kantian abstractions into the teeming convulsive world from which Darwin would derive the principle of natural selection: "Schopenhauer marks then, in the history of thought, the transition from romantic idealism to modern realism, the return to the natural order." [26]

Surveying the tradition that begins with Kant, Royce says: "The early idealists, then, made the problems of philosophy center about two principal conceptions, that of the self and that of the Absolute." [27] He was in their debt for doing so. They gave him the lead suggested by the title of his magnum opus, *The World and the Individual.*

He found something useful in every member of the tradition, and his fellow-feeling for them continues undisguised no matter how much extraneous material he may import into his absolute idealism from other sources. The importation he found indispensable because his German predecessors had never made their theorizing either logical enough or empirical enough. His purpose became to vindicate post-Kantian metaphysics by taking it into his philosophical laboratory, expunging its excrescences, and supporting its essentials with stronger materials that had been developed by more recent thinkers.

II *New Tools of Thought*

Royce's era was one of great intellectual excitement. Almost all of the sciences and humanities were developing in revolutionary ways with dizzying speed. It is hard to believe, but a number of masters who seem so contemporary with us of the mid-twentieth century had already established their reputations well within Royce's lifetime: Einstein, Planck, Freud, Jung, Bergson, Russell, Dewey, Picasso, Stravinsky, Frank Lloyd Wright. These men bridged the gap between Victorian ideas and those that we take to be specifically of the twentieth century.

Royce should be classed with them. He was a contemporary of Lotze, who died in 1881, and of Dewey, who died in 1958; and he understood the transition in philosophy that led from the one to the other. He was familiar with the work of Bergson and Russell, which he tried to incorporate, insofar as he agreed with it, into his own system. He knew and said that logic and science were at a crisis in their histories. He just missed relativity and psychoanalysis.

Of the names mentioned, Royce's ignorance of Picasso, Stravinsky, and Wright harmed him little; for the novel forms of art, music, and architecture could not have added much to his philosophical system. His unawareness of the physicists and psychologists *did* harm his theorizing since he might have used relativity and quantum theory, as Eddington soon would, to support a quasi-Kantian version of the philosophy of science; and, he might have appropriated psychoanalysis, in its Jungian form at any rate, for his theory of the self and the community.

Of the two branches of psychology, philosophical and experimental, Royce was really interested in the former. The idealistic metaphysics, as he pointed out, made the self the center of philosophy; and, from Kant on, philosophers had been discussing with increasing depth and refinement the meaning of self-consciousness, the relations between intellect and will, and sundry other problems of a distinctly psychological character.

Such was Royce's type of philosophizing. *The World and the Individual* is largely philosophical psychology, and some of his essays and articles are almost entirely so: "The Implications of Self-consciousness," "Anomolies of Self-consciousness," "Self-consciousness, Social Consciousness and Nature," "Originality and Consciousness." Royce here follows Kant and the post-Kantians in their effort to probe ever deeper into the roots of personality; and much of what he says is simply a result of introspection and the epistemological analysis of its evidence. His leading questions are "What is it to be conscious?" and "What does self-consciousness imply?" [28]

The close union of psychology and idealist philosophy had not persisted among scientific psychologists. Royce's older contemporaries—Brentano, Stumpf, Müller, Ebbinghaus—felt a profound aversion for absolutistic modes of thought when they were studying human nature in their psychological laboratories. They made part of the general scientific consensus of the later nineteenth century that the post-Kantians had been bizarre if not mad, and that science should decontaminate itself of the idealist mythologies.

Yet, what the psychologists objected to was not philosophy as such, but this dominant brand of philosophizing. They could not abide Hegel; but even laboratory work was forcing a realization that the evidence of experimental research needed to be clarified by philosophical concepts. The moral emerged that, since psychology could not get along without philosophy or with idealist philosophy, a better philosophy was needed. The nineteenth-century associationism, which pretended to be scientific because it postulated "atoms" of sensation coalescing under laws analogous to the behavior of actual atoms in the Newtonian system, was completely shattered. Other schools of psychology emerged—among them, Brentano's act psychology, the Gestalt psychology of Wertheimer and Kohler, and, most important of all, psychoanalysis, which itself became a philosophy for its adepts.

Royce saw that philosophical psychology had to be reinstated. Noting that "sooner or later psychology and philosophy must join hands afresh," he says: "As a fact, I myself can find no hostility between the psychological interpretation of consciousness and the philosophical interpretation of reality in terms of consciousness."[29] What he took exception to was the anti-idealism of the psychologists. What he set out to do was to keep his idealism, and to prove that it alone made sense of psychology.

There is no difficulty about how he would have interpreted act psychology, Gestalt psychology, and psychoanalysis. All three are based on the synthetic power of the self, on the subjective factor that unconsciously unifies experience and gives it meaning. Royce would unhesitatingly have "placed" this factor in the older philosophical thought: He would have identified it as Kant's spontaneity of the understanding, no matter how disparately the three psychologies might understand it, no matter what specific operations they might attribute to it. Royce would have told the psychologists from Brentano to Freud what he told James, that they were all implicitly metaphysical idealists.

Royce spoke to psychologists as a professional. He served as president of the American Psychological Association, and as chairman of its Committee on Apparitions and Haunted Houses, which, at his prompting changed its title to the Committee on Phantasms and Presentiments. He wrote a textbook (*Outlines of Psychology*), many reviews of books on the subject (including one of James's *Principles*), and several long articles with self-evident titles like "The New Psychology and the Consulting

Psychologist," "Preliminary Report on Imitation," "Hallucination of Memory and 'Telepathy'" and "On Certain Psychological Aspects of Moral Training."

If these are perfunctory writings that do not give Royce any standing in the history of psychology, they help to fill in the picture of his mind; and they show that he was not imperceptive of the drift of the science. His empirical bent led him into laboratories and haunted houses, both of which institutions are still standing, albeit not with equal stability. Unconvinced by the occult, he counseled further investigation of extrasensory perception along the lines now pursued at the Duke University laboratory of parapsychology. He seems an incipient psychoanalyst when, remarking on how much psychologists know about the sane and the insane, he asks his colleagues to accumulate more data on the type that stands in between—"the fantastic man, the dreamer." [30]

Little of this was in any sense new. Royce had learned, and continued to learn, from the great psychologists. He must have heard Lotze lecture on physiological psychology—Lotze, who was famous for his theory of local signs, the theory that what seems to be a direct perception of spatial depth is mainly an inference from the movement of the eye muscles and the angle of vision on the retina. Royce worked with Münsterberg at Harvard on the psychology of imitation and the practical origin of ideas. At Princeton, James Mark Baldwin was expounding a theory like Royce's about the social origin of personality. Royce picked up ideas from his reading of Wundt, Marbe, Brentano, Ribot.

But it goes without saying that the master-influence on Royce the psychologist was William James. Royce's "A New Study of Psychology" is a highly favorable review of the *Principles of Psychology.* Royce admired James's insight into the formation of habits, the function of volition in conduct, the nature of the higher thought processes. Defending James for saying that attention often determines pleasure and pain rather than the reverse, Royce trembles on the brink of the psychology that would soon come out of Vienna: "A fixed idea may be a painful one, and usually is so. Yet it persists, and *just because it is painful.*" [31]

Most of all, Royce took from James the description of how our knowledge is constructed by the specious present which we catch momentarily as it slips from the future into the past, and by the limitation of span to which our faculties are confined. Royce knew what Kant and the post-Kantians had done with the idea of the finite self hemmed in by its own subjective conditions. James, although far removed from the idealists, gave a scientific explanation of the fact: We cannot grasp more than a small fragment of reality at any one time, and that fragment is determined by our choice from the flux around us. Royce accepts this in a more profound sense. He holds that involuntary inattention on the part of the finite self, the only thing that bars us from infinite knowledge, is "the original sin, as it were, with which our form of consciousness is beset." [32] Conversely, the Absolute can be defined as the being that suffers from no such inability to notice everything. The result of Royce's philosophical analysis of this psychological fact is what Gabriel Marcel has aptly termed "a metaphysics of attention." [33]

Anyone familiar with Royce's approach to philosophy will anticipate his verdict on the *Principles of Psychology*: The stream of thought and the fragmentariness of experience are declared to be ultimately inexplicable except as elements of an absolute metaphysical idealism.

Six years later, writing on philosophy in America for German readers, Royce explained the current relation between psychology and philosophy: "American philosophy may long remain, upon one side, Hegelian; it is sure, however, to become also psychological in its interests and its methods." [34] He was prescient when he said this. Even John Dewey was something of a Hegelian at the start of his career; and psychology exerted an increasing impact on philosophy until the extravagances of psychoanalysis and the absurdities of behaviorism forced a reaction.

Royce retained both Hegel and psychology. He remained a philosophical psychologist. The only lasting part of his psychology is that which he integrated into his philosophy.

Royce was interested in psychology not only for the sake of metaphysics but for the sake of logic. One of his best articles is called "Recent Logical Inquiries and their Psychological Bearings." Delivered originally as the presidential address before the American Psychological Association in 1902, this article quickly moves away from the experimental psychology of Ribot,

Marbe, Erdmann, and Wundt, and proposes that psychology undertake to throw light on the logic of Klein's theory of space, Poincaré's theory of material groups, and Pearson's theory of scientific explanation. Royce wants to unify different disciplines through a "comparative morphology of concepts."[35]

He had, of course, been interested in logic since his student days, and more particularly since he had written his *Primer of Logical Analysis for the Use of Composition Students.* He did not become a skilled expert until Peirce advised him to become one: "Mr. Charles Peirce wrote to me, in a letter of kindly acknowledgment, the words: 'But when I read you, I do wish that you would study logic. You need it so much.' "[36] Royce took Peirce's advice. He made himself systematically acquainted with the masters of symbolic logic: Sigwart, Schroeder, Boole, Jevons, Kempe, Russell, Whitehead–and Peirce. He wrote hundreds of pages about this new phase of Western thought, not only using it in his books, but also dealing with special interests of his in a succession of essays: "The Principles of Logic," "The Relation of the Principles of Logic to the Foundations of Geometry," "An Extension of the Algebra of Logic," "Axiom," "Negation," "Order," and others.

Royce utilized logic to sustain his philosophy in the three major realms of the theory of infinity, the theory of interpretation, and the theory of order.

The theory of infinity came to Royce as an extension of modern mathematics mainly due to Cantor and Dedekind, who were concerned with the distinction between finite and infinite numbers. Cantor arrived at the definition of an infinite number as a number that can be put into a one-to-one correspondence with a part of itself. The now-familiar example is the relation of the whole number series to the series of even numbers, where the latter marches with the former, number by number, to infinity:

1	2	3	4	5	6	7	8	9	10 . . .
2	4	6	8	10	12	14	16	18	20 . . .

The whole is equal to the part. This is a peculiar characteristic of infinite numbers.

Royce took the idea and generalized it to cover non-mathematical classes. His definition of infinity is: "An object or a system is infinite if it can be rightly regarded as capable of being precisely represented, in complexity of structure, by one of its own parts."[37] The object or system is then what is called self-representative.

The importance of the theory of infinite numbers for Royce is that he thought it escaped the logical strictures that were being brought against the idea of individual things subsisting with the Absolute. Bradley argued that an actual infinite could only be self-contradictory, that the relations of things in the world involved an actual infinite, and that therefore both relations and objects must be illusory—appearance rather than reality. The heart of his argument is that if two objects are related, then each object must be related to the relation, which produces an infinite regress.

Royce devoted the long appendix in the first volume of *The World and the Individual* to a refutation of this part of Bradley's *Appearance and Reality*. The refutation hangs on the thought that, even if an infinity of relations be admitted, that is nothing against their reality because an infinite system is not self-contradictory. The infinite, as the mathematicians have shown, does not do away with its parts, but rather presupposes them.

Royce's favorite example is a map laid on the surface of England, representing everything on that surface, and therefore itself as well. The infinity here (theoretical rather than actual, according to Royce, only because of technical difficulties) is the succession of endless maps, one inside the other. Varying the image, Royce adduces the type of label that offers a representation of the package on which it is stuck, including itself, so that there is a kind of Chinese-box procession to infinity.[38] He insists that the infinity is necessitated, or else the representation is faulty. The actual infinite not only may, but must, be.

From Dedekind, Royce took an especially significant case of the actual infinite—the relation of thoughts and objects. This example begins with the self-representative aspect and infers the infinite. There is an idea for every object such that they stand in a one-to-one correspondence. But ideas are objects (we can have an idea of an idea). Hence the whole class of objects (things plus ideas) is in a one-to-one correspondence with its part (ideas alone). This is an actual infinite according to the definition. Royce pursues Dedekind's argument to the notion that complete self-consciousness would be completely self-representative, therefore infinite. He ends with the conclusion: "I believe it to be demonstrable that the real universe is an exactly determinate but actually infinite system, whose structure is that revealed to us in Self-consciousness." [39] Complete self-consciousness = the Absolute.

The theory of infinity leads into the theory of interpretation. Royce derives from Peirce the analysis of knowledge by which, to the perception of particulars and the conception of universals, is added the interpretation of signs. The third intellectual process is described by both Peirce and Royce as the only way of accounting for our knowledge of the minds of other men, which are neither particulars perceived nor universals conceived. This interpretation of signs involves the triad of sign, interpreter, and interpretee—for example, foreign language, translator, and reader.

Interpretation touches infinity because each operation is itself a sign, so that the progression is potentially endless and can be actually ended only by the introduction of some outside influence. A translation is a sign that can be interpreted further, but generally the reader who understands it will call a halt by voluntarily foregoing further interpretation since his purpose of understanding is accomplished.

Interpretation is a system that uniquely relates to time and the self. The sign pertains to the past; the interpreter, to the present; the interpretee, to the future. The self performs all three functions when the past self is interpreted by the present self to the future self. Similarly, human beings interpret one another, and so make social life possible. The theory of interpretation covers even the Absolute, for an interpretation is an act of will, the development of "an infinite multitude out of the expression of a single purpose," and complete self-consciousness is supremely capable of doing just that.[40]

Interpretation therefore implies communal existence, and that is the reason for Royce's statement, which seems so odd at first glance, that the self, the world, and the Absolute are all communities of interpretation. He infers that "the system of metaphysics which is needed to define the constitution of this world of interpretation must be the generalized theory of an ideal society." [41]

Royce built such a system of metaphysics. The theories of infinity and interpretation ramified into every corner of his universe of intelligibility.

The problem of the one and the many is solved for him through the idea of a self-representative system, which proves in spite of Bradley that relations are real rather than impossible. As the number series does not negate the reality of its parts, the Absolute does not negate the independent existence of finite things. In neither case is endless counting implied, or the vain attempt to locate a final term. It is a question of definition, plan, will; and if the world we know is a definition or plan or will of the Absolute, then the actuality of that world is not merely postulated but guaranteed.

Royce proposes through this metaphysics to avoid both monism and pluralism, or rather to unite what is true in both theories—to evade the all-encompassing one that admits of no distinctions, and the many that has no principle of unity. Ubiquitous spirituality is the answer. The individual becomes a community of interpretation by unifying his experience through time. When many individuals do the same for their corporate experience, society arises: "And, if in ideal, we aim to conceive the divine nature, how better can we conceive it than in the form of the Community of Interpretation, and above all in the form of the Interpreter, who interprets all to all, and each individual to the world, and the world of spirits to each individual?" [42]

Having stated the ideal in this passage, Royce proceeds to argue for its reality on the ground that interpretation being real, its conditions must be real. The thought is so comprehensive in its import that Marcel can say: "We thus understand that for Royce interpretation is the main business of philosophy." [43]

The theory of order is the logical principle that allows Royce most scope for developing a "comparative morphology of concepts." Working on the basis laid down by the British logician A. B. Kempe, Royce applies the idea to everything in heaven and earth. He knew that much had been done to produce a unified science: arithmetic joined to geometry (Descartes), mathematics joined to logic (Frege, Russell, Whitehead), logic joined to the philosophy of science (Poincaré, Peirce). Royce thought that further discoveries of the same type remained to be made. He defines logic as "The Science of Order" and sets before contemporary thinkers the task to be attacked:

> It is, therefore, not a matter of mere accident or mere play on words, that, if a man publishes a book called simply "A Treatise on Order," or "The Doctrine of Order," we cannot tell from the title whether it is a treatise on social problems, or on preserving an orderly social order against anarchy, or on studying those unsymmetrical and transitive relations, those operations and correlations, upon which the theories of arithmetical, geometrical and logical order depend. The bridge that should connect our logic and mathematics with our social theories is still unfinished.[44]

Royce intended to be the architect of the bridge, and the builder of at least some of the foundation and superstructure. His most incongruous addition to it is his theory of insurance, his belief that international order might be achieved through the interpretive triad of policy holder, beneficiary, and insurance company. The notion hardly seems philosophical or even serious, but Royce became solemnly occupied with it when he was meditating on the quest for peace during World War I: It is the burden of *War and Insurance* and of "The Possibility of International Insurance" in *The Hope of the Great Community*.

There is a deeper difficulty than incongruity in Royce's application of logic to life. His argument against the critical rationalists, that they confuse reality and possibility, is one that can be turned against himself. He falls into a fallacy by imagining that a "definite" infinite can be equated with an "actual" infinite. The mathematical infinite is definite but not actual since, while it gives a formula that can be applied without limit, the application to infinity is never fulfilled. Aristotle's analysis of the relation of a line to its points is relevant here: The number of points on a line is potentially infinite; the number actualized is always finite. A. E. Taylor, who is not unsympathetic to Royce's idealism, presents the difficulty in a few words: "The fundamental defect in Professor Royce's reasoning seems to me to lie in the tacit transition from the notion of an infinite *series* to that of an infinite completed *sum*."[45]

Peirce goes farther in isolating "Prof. Royce's greatest fault as a philosophical thinker":

> Metaphysicians have always taken mathematics as their exemplar in reasoning, without remarking the essential difference between that science and their own. Mathematical reasoning has for its object to ascertain what would be true in a hypothetical world which the mathematician has created for himself—not altogether arbitrarily, it is true, but nevertheless, so that it can contain no element which he has not himself deliberately introduced into it. All that his sort of reasoning, therefore, has to do is develop a preconceived idea; and it never reaches any conclusion at all as to what is or is not true of the world of existences.[46]

Royce reads into his infinite much more than is revealed by mathematical logic, and that is why he is able to carry the infinite chain of interpretations, only potential for Peirce, into an elaborate metaphysics. But by the same token, the "much more" could still be sound even if this particular argument is not. Roycean idealism is neither proven nor disproven by generalized mathematics. Royce's logic is more important per se than for its bearing on his metaphysics.

Naturally Royce went to the physical sciences for data to incorporate into his system of philosophy. He thought it safe to do so because the enormous expansion of the laboratory disciplines like physics and geology had garnered enough indubitable truths about nature to correct the vagaries of *Naturphilosophie*. He would balance Fichte, Schelling, and Hegel with Peirce, Enriques, and Poincaré. He thought that the latter three were going in his direction, if they but realized it: "What science seeks is essentially what we are seeking—to catch the rhythm and the very pulse-beat of the reason that is and must be, amid all the caprice of nature, yes, even because of this wealth of caprice in nature, at the very heart of the world. We return to the world of science then, to enrich its postulates by our idealistic interpretation, and to enrich our own too abstract fashion of conceiving the rationality of things through the wealth of nature's facts." [47]

It could be surmised that what actually concerns Royce is not science so much as the philosophy of science. Writing at length about evolution, he mentions scientists like Lyell, Darwin, and von Baer; but he does so only to note how far they support an idealist metaphysics of evolution. He makes more of Peirce, who gives him a statistical explanation not only of evolution but of natural laws in general.[48] Peirce is also the source of Royce's belief that inductive reasoning means testing hypotheses by sampling.[49]

Among the minor works of Royce are the introductions he wrote to *Problems of Science* by Federigo Enriques and *The Foundations of Science* by Henri Poincaré. Enriques was for Royce an antidote to Bergson—a plausible advocate of intellect over instinct in scientific thought, an admirable seeker after synthesis of science, and a good example of the comparative methodologist.[50] Poincaré was for Royce, and probably for most scientists and philosophers, the most creative philosopher of science then at work. Royce praises the French thinker for rendering obsolete the crude cosmological speculations of Herbert Spencer and for opening a new path to scientific understanding by proving that scientific principles, while not arbitrary, often transcend experience, and rightly transcend it because otherwise science would be impossible, condemned to do without the fructifying ideas that rise out of imaginative intelligence. Royce finds a resemblance between Poincaré and Kant: Poincaré's unverifiable but necessary hypotheses are the counterpart of Kant's regulative principles.[51]

The mention of Kant is apposite. Having mastered what symbolic logic and mathematics and the philosophy of science had to say, Royce could turn back to the philosophy that had been his all along. He would develop that philosophy with a wealth of detail, but without disavowing any of its fundamentals. He remains Kantian in his pursuit of the conditions of experience. He remains the ethical idealist of his Fichtean period. He quotes Peirce on the fact that the self is not a datum, but he had read something very like this theory in Hegel. If he puts interpretation in place of the Hegelian dialectic and science in place of Schelling's *Naturphilosophie,* his doing so does not compromise his earlier allegiance to Hegel and Schelling. He may now define his ultimate reality as an infinite community of interpretation; but, for all that, it remains identifiably the post-Kantian Absolute.

In sum, Royce enjoins logic on the idealists and idealism on the logicians, and he warns each group that it cannot comprehend its own thought without assimilating that of the other.

III *Method*

With the historical positions formulated, and the relevance to them of the latest modes of thought, the problem of method remains. "A philosophy must indeed be judged not by its theses, but by its methods," as Royce puts it.[52] A true conclusion has no warrant if it comes at the end of a piece of defective reasoning, while a sound technique remains valuable even though the thinker may in fact have drawn illogical conclusions. Royce's intent is to put true conclusions and sound technique together so that his metaphysics may be invulnerable at either end.

Methodology has, of course, been a preoccupation of philosophers throughout the modern era. Royce finds satisfactory reasons—satisfactory to him at least—for rejecting all the methods except those in agreement with the idealistic tradition, and especially with Kant and the post-Kantians. Descartes' methodical doubt leading to the *cogito* ("I think therefore I am") is, after Fichte, set aside because the "I" is a first problem and not a first principle of philosophy. Spinoza's mathematical treatment of metaphysics is too abstract to be explanatory of empirical reality. James goes to the other extreme with his pragmatism and becomes so enmeshed in practical results, and on a personal level, that he cannot distinguish between fact and fantasy.

Perhaps Aristotelian realism, with its commitment to both fact and logic, might be the answer? Why not meet the facts with an open mind and see what they have to say for themselves? Because they speak stridently, not with a single voice, or even like a chorus, but in a crescendo of individual arias that often do not sound as if they came from a single composition.

Royce holds that the extramental world is simply too complicated to offer an entrée into metaphysics. Experience assails us in a bewildering profusion that seems chaotic in its multiplicity and variety. Everywhere we find the apparently gratuitous existence of things that come and go, often with haphazard contingency, as we look around. Ants and stars and other men and moral values and aesthetic emotions—how can these be unified by an inspection of their objective natures? The many empirical theories from materialism to pragmatism prove for Royce that no such unification of the world of facts can be achieved.

The correct method must begin on the other side of the knowing process. Things may be opaque; thoughts are clear. And so, like Plato and Berkeley, like Kant and Hegel, Royce will begin with thoughts. His method is the way of ideas rather than the way of facts. "I am," he says, "one of those who hold that when you ask the question: What is an Idea? and: How can ideas stand in any true relation to Reality? you attack the world-knot in the way that promises most for the untying of its meshes." [53]

Royce uses this general idealistic method in three special forms: He seeks to establish his philosophy through the principles of consistency, dialectic, and synthesis.

Consistency as such is not the property of idealism. It forms the basis of Aristotle's realism in both logic and metaphysics, where it is defined as the law of thought called the principle of contradiction: "Nothing can both be and not be at the same time and in the same respect." Indeed, consistency applies more to things than to thoughts; for, while *things* cannot contradict one another, *thoughts* both can and often do. But realists and idealists alike would agree that where contradiction occurs, something is wrong; and it is on this primary level that Royce launches his investigation. He "experiments" with judgments to show that some are proven to be true when they are denied, because otherwise a contradiction in the Aristotelian sense would result.

Suppose that I say: "There are no true judgments." My judgment purports to be true, and therefore the fact that there *are* true judgments is sustained. This manner of turning a false judgment against itself, of revealing the suicidal tendency of sophisms, is characteristic of Royce. The following passage from "The Principles of Logic" is basic for him:

> There are *some* truths that are known *not* by virtue of special successes which this or that hypothesis obtains in particular instances, but by virtue of the fact that there are certain modes of activity, certain laws of the rational will, which we reinstate and verify, through the very act of attempting to presuppose that

> these modes of activity do not exist, or that these laws are not valid. Thus, whoever says that there are no classes whatever in his world, inevitably classifies.[54]

No logician will impugn Royce's logic at this point. Controversy arises when Royce proceeds to impress his theory of consistency into the service of his idealistic metaphysics—when he argues that the denial of idealism proves idealism to be true.

He is the grateful heir of Kant, and more explicitly of Hegel, from whom descends the habit of thus extending consistency into an idealistic theory of reality. Kant foreshadows the development in modern logic of the coherence theory of truth by which verities are not independent but gain their validity by cohering with a whole complexus of others. Not self-evidence but mutual combination is the guarantee of judgments. Consistency of the Kantian type is the rationale of Hegelian metaphysics, for which truths are so intimately related that there is no explaining any one of them short of integrating it into the cosmic Absolute.

Since Royce agrees with Hegel, the former has been made the target of the criticisms aimed at the latter, in particular of the criticism that a single truth does not actually imply all other truths. The word "truth" is notoriously difficult to deal with, but this much may be said: The principle of consistency is not usually accepted by modern logicians in its Hegelian or Roycean forms.[55] This is another place where Royce reads more into his premises than they contain.

The application of the principle of consistency leads to dialectic in Royce's method. Dialectic is for him a means of proving that idealism is true because consistent and that non-idealistic systems are false because inconsistent. The Roycean dialectic is not Hegelian: It does not move by thesis, antithesis, and synthesis. Royce's gravamen against Hegel is that the Hegelian dialectic cannot account for science or natural philosophy, falls short of Hegel's claim of universality, and is no substitute for modern logic and scientific method. It remains, where useful, a special case of interpretation. What is truly Hegelian in Royce is the resolute search for contradictions in opposing views, and a too-facile readiness to believe them found.

Royce at times handles dialectic more in the manner of Plato. He allows ideas as much room for maneuver as possible to see if they survive or die, whether by murder or suicide. One problem is handled almost identically by the two thinkers, the problem of the one and the many. The Platonic dialogue *Parmenides* argues that the monistic One of the Eleatics is self-contradictory because, if it exists, then so do at least two realities, the One and its being. Royce attacks Eleaticism on the ground that it implies at least the two realities of the One and the idea of the One.[56]

The three philosophies on which Royce turns his dialectic most often are the philosophies of realism, mysticism, and critical rationalism. His indictment is that each presupposes principles and truths contradictory to its overtly stated doctrine.

Realism is right insofar as it accepts the reality of things outside the finite knowing mind and controlling knowledge—that is, realism is right because it agrees with idealism. But realism claims to be based on experience, and experience presents no such utterly independent objects as those postulated by realism. Looking at it another way, realism slights relations, which are just as objective as the things they connect. Moreover, the realistic theory, "being an idea, and at the same time an independent entity, has no relation to any real world of the sort that the theory defines."[57]

Mysticism is an improvement on realism because it does not sunder idea and object; on the contrary, it stipulates their union as firmly as does idealism. Although usually a doctrine of religious experience, mysticism is not so defined by Royce; for him its essential meaning is that reality is apprehended in an immediate intuition, whether sensory or emotional or intellectual: "No matter what object the mystic seems to call real. That might be from your point of view any subject you please; yourself, or God, or the wall."[58] Mysticism is therefore pure empiricism: "The mystic loves the simple fact just so far as it is simple and unmediated, the absolute datum, with no question to be asked."[59]

Where lies the fallacy of mysticism? It lies in the supposition that discursive reasoning can be by-passed through an appeal to pure experience. The mystic invariably invokes the logical processes that he affects to despise, and his ultimate reality is apprehended at the end of a chain of thought, the links of which must be real too: "What is, is not then *merely* immediate, is not merely the limit of the finite series, is not merely the zero of consciousness. The result therefore is that Immediacy is but one aspect of Being." [60]

Critical rationalism is a further stride toward complete idealism. Stemming from Kant's notion of possible experience, forming the heart of the axiologies of Münsterberg, Windelband, and Rickert, and much affected by philosophers of science who call a halt too soon in the philosophizing, critical rationalism explains both the *objects* of realism and the *object* of mysticism by incorporating them into the theory that reality is what validates or could validate ideas.

This is a value-philosophy. Facts are what give worth to thoughts, the manner in which they do so being analogous to the operation of certain axiological elements in civilized life. The cosmos may be compared to a bank on which checks are drawn, and in which there must be a specific bank account if a given check is to be honored. That is why validity is made into the criterion of truth, for reality is said to validate true ideas as a bank validates a good check; reality exposes false ideas as a bank bounces a rubber check.

The critical rationalists thought that they had discovered the touchstone of criteriology, that they could extend the axiological principle into every department of thought and experience—interpreting metaphysics, mathematics, and science according to the rationale of financial systems, class-behavior, and the moral law. Everything is from them a matter of credit.

The scientific interpretation of the theory appealed to scientists for obvious reasons. It seemed almost self-evident that laboratory experiment resembles banking. One develops a theory and tests it against the facts to see whether they validate it, just as one takes a check to the bank to find out whether it is genuine or not. Moreover, there is no appeal from the verdict in either case: There is no more sense in supporting a false theory by manipulating the facts than there is in demanding payment on a bad check.

We have already noted Royce's fundamental objection to critical rationalism: It confuses actuality and possibility. The stability of the metaphysical "bank" is suspect. There is no way of telling what is in the "vault" which no one has inspected, how long "checks" will continue to be honored, or how close the "institution" is to closing its doors. In the case of any real bank, an audit can satisfy us whether it is sound or not. But who "audits" the universe?

To drop the figure of speech, Royce opposes critical rationalism for presuming that actuality and possibility are on the same level of ontological reality. If it properly makes experience the criterion, it improperly appeals to possible experience wherever validation has not been effectively carried out—which is like accepting the actuality of money in the bank vault just because of the possibility that it may be there.

The dialectical history of this system as followed by Royce reveals its suicidal tendency, for validity in the sense intended inevitably points beyond itself and thereby exposes the self-contradiction that undermines it from within. Consider the astronomer who forms a hypothesis about a hitherto unknown star in the sky: He focuses his telescope on the spot where he thinks it must be, and finds that it is indeed there. Critical rationalism is so far correct in stating that reality has validated his idea. But what about the multitude of stars that will never be discovered, and will therefore never make any astronomical ideas true?

> In brief, What is a valid or a determinately possible experience at the moment when it is supposed to be only possible? What is a valid truth at the moment when nobody verifies its validity? When we ourselves find the possible experience, it is something living, definite—yes, individual. When we ourselves verify a valid assertion, it is again something that plays a part in our individual process of living and observing. But when we speak of such truths as barely valid, as merely possible objects of experience, they appear once more as mere universals. Can these universals, not yet verified, consistently be regarded as possessing wholeness of Being? [61]

They cannot because, to return to the astronomical instance, the aim is to discover a real star with real characteristics—definite size, weight, density, temperature, distance, velocity, etc. A bare definition that fits all stars and identifies none will not content any astronomer.

This is the point at which critical rationalism, systematically thought out, becomes absolute idealism. The dichotomy between actual experience and possible experience is surmounted by Royce's theory that unvalidated possibilities exist only for finite minds. All experience must be actual to some knower somewhere. Who "audits" the universe? The Absolute.

Speaking summarily of the three philosophies that need only to be corrected to be sound, Royce says: "What is, is authoritative over against finite ideas, as Realism asserted; is one with the true meaning of the idea, as Mysticism insisted; and is valid, as Critical Rationalism demanded." [62]

The adherents of the three schools obviously would not endorse Royce's dialectic. Perhaps they all would repeat James's rejoinder (spoken of Royce's realist), that Royce sets up a straw man with just those intellectual defects that can most easily be caricatured, so that his grandiose "refutation" misses the point. However that may be—and granted that Royce has the typical metaphysician's ability to turn logic into logic-chopping when the argument becomes over-sophisticated—as far as his definitions reflect "pure" positions, he is a sure-footed mental gymnast walking the dialectical tightrope amid the contrasting philosophies around him. He is not simply negative. He has dealt with some of his opponents, although the number may not be so great as he imagines. His dialectic is a powerful example of philosophical thinking. Peirce libeled two philosophers when he wrote that "Dr. Royce cannot free himself from the Hegelian notion that the one satisfactory method in philosophy is to examine an opinion and to detect in it some hidden denial of itself—which is nothing but the *reductio ad absurdum*." [63]

Once the competing systems are out of the way, once they have been shown to be internally inconsistent and therefore dialectically unstable, and once the intimations of idealism in them have been made manifest, then Royce is ready to show that idealism, which unites their truths, is at the same time internally consistent. To achieve this he uses the method of synthesis, ranging across experience and its conditions, accumulating multiple proofs that idealism can account for everything including itself.

His thought is essentially relational. He hunts for orders, classes, groups, and communities that will unify individual things and persons. He constructs a pattern of philosophical explanation in which everything finds its proper place in relation to everything else. His application of the phrase "absolute pragmatist" to himself is a paradigm of his attitude. He thinks that the two theories can be made coherent in a single system. So can all of the great philosophical dichotomies, the terms of which have so often been called mutually exclusive: Idea and object, thought and volition, finite and infinite, time and eternity, freedom and determinism, the one and the many—and these are only a selection from his list. His is a "synoptic vision." [64]

Royce will take any idea and universalize it. He will examine its relations, classify and order it, and then let it tell him whether it coheres with the rest of the pattern. If it does, it is true; if not, false. Scientific ideas are a case in point: "It is our own reflective interest that has now suggested to us the mere experiment of seeing whether the conceptions that these inductions involve are capable of being universalized, of being pressed to the limit, and whether they remain coherent when this is hypothetically done. The purpose of the experiment is to see whether the world as it seems to outer experience can really be viewed as a fair specimen of the world as it really is." [65]

The explication of the highest metaphysical ideas in exactly this sense is Royce's vocation in philosophy.

CHAPTER *4*

Absolute Idealism

ROYCE was a philosopher in the grand manner. By his efforts at system building he entered the western tradition of Aristotle, Aquinas, Kant, Hegel. He aspired to put a comparable treatise on the shelves beside the *Metaphysics,* the *Summa Theologica,* the *Critique of Pure Reason,* and the *Logic.* To say that he fell short of these masters, and that *The World and the Individual* does not match their finest works, is no denigration; to say that he bears at least a limited comparison to them, and he does, is to place a high valuation on his achievement.

Royce deals with most of the standard departments of philosophy: logic, epistemology, metaphysics, psychology, ethics, axiology, the history of philosophy, the philosophy of science. He handles almost all the perennial problems of philosophy: the analysis of experience, the categories of thought, the criterion of truth, the nature of the self, the structure of the cosmos, the problem of evil, the relation of finite and infinite. He writes voluminously about all of them, for he is no more a man of one book than the philosophers mentioned above.

In spite of the technical orientation that Royce brought to the study of philosophical ideas—in spite of his eagerness to appropriate the latest theories and theorems, in spite of his determination to learn from thinkers he found sympathetic and his willingness to learn from those antipathetic to him—one need not be an historian of philosophy, a psychologist, or a mathematical logician to understand his system. His metaphysics can be formulated in explicitly metaphysical terms, and, whatever the extraneous supports with which he may shore it up, stands or falls accordingly to explicitly metaphysical criteria.

Again, Royce is not an intellectually disjointed philosopher of the kind who quarrels with himself from book to book. It is proper to look for stages in his mental biography; to look for totally new beginnings is fruitless, for there are none. Hegel said of Schelling that he "conducted his philosophical studies in public" because of Schelling's habit of rushing his latest notions into print without pausing to ask whether they jibed with what he had already presented to his readers as the ultimate philosophy. Royce, the direct opposite of Schelling, is ever-mindful of what he has said in the past. Adding something at each stage, he takes back nothing of substance. The growth of his thought is organic, from within.

Furthermore, Royce writes philosophy with a skilled hand and with a disciplined comprehension of exactly what he wants to say. He is one of the most repetitive philosophers, not from poverty of thought or arrested development, but because the same problems keep coming up in different contexts: Having satisfied himself, once and for all, about the correct solution to a given problem, he must perforce repeat the solution as often as the problem confronts him. The logical pattern of his problems-and-solutions has the same undeviating character, so that his system is no more variable than its elements. His theory of the Absolute, to mention the clearest instance, appears in *The Religious Aspect of Philosophy* (1885) and reappears like a friendly guide throughout his publications down to *The Problem of Christianity* (1913).

This is not a system that gives the experts elbow room for their great delight, the formulation of opposing interpretations arrived at through the ambiguities of the philosopher or the subjective insights of his critics. Certain details can be and are debated; but there never will be disputatious schools of Royceans comparable to the Hegelians or the Marxists. Royce has explained himself at length in large treatises as well as succinctly in essays, articles, and letters. With so much assistance from the philosopher himself, his critics are pretty much agreed about the essentials of his philosophy, no matter how radically they may disagree about the value of that philosophy.

I *The Meaning of Ideas*

Royce's method being that of idealism, by which experience is to be interpreted from the side of ideas rather than facts, one great riddle presents itself on the threshold of his philosophical inquiry: What is an idea?

By common consent of philosophers and laymen, and taking the term in the broadest definition to include both sense perceptions and abstract thoughts, an idea is a cognitive act that reflects objective reality in the mind. An idea of a chair is a mental representation of the chair as it exists extramentally. Royce accepts this definition—as the first word on the subject. True as far as it goes, it does not go far enough for Royce the voluntarist, who adds that an idea always and of necessity has a volitional element. He joins the Kantians, the pragmatists, and the empirical psychologists in holding that an idea is a "plan of action" because it always involves not only reflection of the object but also response by the subject: "Intelligent ideas then, belong, so to speak, to the motor side of your life rather than to the merely sensory. This was what Kant meant by the spontaneity of the understanding." [1]

A stark momentary sensation breaking in on the mental processes is not an idea—the immediate reaction of the nerves that follows from, say, a door slamming or a sudden pain. It takes volition supervening upon sensation to generate an idea. When one decides to get up and fasten the door, or to sit still in the knowledge that it has fastened itself, or to adopt any other attitude toward it, *then* one has an idea of the door. A pain, similarly, becomes an idea only when it has provoked some purpose in the person who feels it, some plan of action with regard to it (the action can, of course, be simply subjective and negative, like a resolve to forget about it and see if it goes away).

There is in Royce's philosophical psychology neither pure cognition nor pure volition: Intellect and will function together. So simple a statement as "I see the dictionary on the table" is inexplicable as an independent sense perception without a conjoined attitude. Every person who makes the statement must entertain some interest in the object, even if only a passing and superficial interest. The deeper the interest, the more patent the volitional element. A lexicographer might mean: "I see a book that I wish to consult." An artist might mean: "I see a juxtaposition of colors that I wish to paint." Their plans of action with regard to the dictionary being different, their ideas of the dictionary are different.

Royce's theory of the idea as purpose is easier to understand from the converse, from the failure of an idea to develop despite the presence of all the non-volitional factors. A man in a reverie may look at the dictionary a dozen times without ever "seeing" it. His attention being elsewhere, his interest in what is before him having lapsed, he forms no idea of the dictionary, no matter how numerous the images carried from its surfaces to his eyes. The physical and physiological factors are powerless until his interest is aroused and his attention focused. Only the volitional bond can span the chasm between subject and object.

Royce's reasoning leads him to define an idea as "any state of consciousness, whether simple or complex, which, when present, is then and there viewed as at least the partial expression or embodiment of a single conscious purpose."[2] Purpose specifies the idea and gives it meaning, objective relevance. Purpose: Idea::Soul:Body.

Yet, the representative function of ideas does seem to be coercive. The dictionary necessarily meets one's eye, granted that attention is at work, and no amount of volition will get around the presence thrust upon one so peremptorily by perception. How is Royce to explain this necessity on the basis of his voluntarism? He does it by one of the master-strokes of his epistemology—by distinguishing between the external meaning and the internal meaning of ideas.

What he means is this. Suppose that the dictionary has a brown color. That is a fact of the objective world and evidently in no way beholden to subjective caprice (the psychology of color-vision by which color *is* subjective is irrelevant here, for no one doubts that there is an objective reason why we see one color rather than another). To take an instance directly from Royce, imagine that one is counting ships in the harbor. Surely, says common sense, the number one arrives at is not a matter of will: There are just so many ships as a real fact, and the counting is correct if it matches the reality, if it truly represents its object. This representative aspect Royce calls the external meaning of ideas.

But consider. It is not enough to have an object on one side of the epistemological bridge, and an idea like it on the other. One may have the idea of the color brown in one's mind without attributing it to any object. One can even say to oneself

"There is a brown dictionary on the table" without getting outside a mere psychological event, an entirely mental phenomenon. In order to make the statement objectively meaningful, the will must be applied in a definite concrete case. One must *intend* to represent *this* dictionary on *this* table. One must say in effect: "I have an idea of a brown dictionary, and there on the table is the one I mean." Only thus can the worth of the statement be judged. Truth lies in the intention, the purpose, the plan of action: "After all, the counting of the ships is valid or invalid *not* alone because of the supposed independent being of the ships, but also because of the conscious act whereby just this collection of ships was first consciously selected for counting. After all, then, no idea is true or false except with reference to the object that this very idea first means to select as its own object." [3] This volitional aspect is what Royce calls the internal meaning of ideas.

The two meanings of meaning lie at the heart of the ontological mystery. On the one hand, the external meaning of the idea, the representative aspect, seems to make the object dominant in the cognitive process: We know what we find in the world around us, not what we wish to find. On the other hand, the internal meaning, the volitional aspect, seems to make the intention dominant: We know what we choose to know. Royce's philosophy is a footnote to his theory of how external and internal meanings are related.

Common sense, in his opinion, burkes the problem by opting as a matter of course for the supremacy of the external meaning, by accepting as self-evident that objects cause ideas, and conversely that ideas resemble objects. Royce objects to the words "cause" and "resemblance." Causation cannot be the answer since there are things we think about that are powerless to exercise the supposed influence on our minds—conspicuously, those in the past (which no longer exist) and those in the future (which do not yet exist). Resemblance cannot be the answer since some ideas obviously do not resemble that to which they refer—conspicuously, mathematical symbols. Although there is no truth without some correspondence between idea and object, the correspondence must be intended, must spring from purpose, and may be very far from a photographic likeness.

If we apply this consideration to the case of the definition of

> truth, we see that, for the first, a true idea, in corresponding to its object, need not in the least be confined to any particular sort or degree of general similarity to its object. The similarity may be as close or as remote, as sensuously interesting or as abstractly formal, as you please. A scientific idea about colors need not be itself a color, not yet an image involving colors. Or, to state the case in a very crude instance, a true idea of a dog need not itself bark in order to be true.[4]

This is the only sense in which Royce is willing to define truth as the agreement between an idea and its object. It is too crude to suppose that objects act on the senses as a stamp acts on wax.

Purpose, then, is basic. The internal meaning of ideas takes precedence over the external meaning, or rather "the external meaning is only apparently external, and, in very truth, is but an aspect of the completely developed internal meaning."[5] The idea is a seeker. It goes outside of itself in search of objective embodiment. It wills its own fulfillment in reality, and succeeds by becoming progressively more determinate. Royce draws a parallel between knowledge in general and the mathematical theory of limits. As the number "two" lies beyond the fractions leading toward it from the number "one," so does the whole of reality lie beyond the human ideas that grasp it in fragments. No matter how precise our ideas may become, they never reflect ultimate being.

This stage of the epistemological analysis concludes with the observation that precision, determination, comes from individual things, not mere generalities. "What is," Royce notes, "or what is real, is as such the complete embodiment, in individual form and in final fulfillment, of the internal meaning of finite ideas."[6] To find such a reality is to find truth itself.

If Royce appears to be talking paradoxically at this point, he is the first to be aware of it. Not afraid to begin with paradox, he has set the stage for a reasoned defense of his systematic metaphysics.

II *From Error to Omniscience*

The ineluctable enigma of Royce's theory is how the internal meaning of an idea can find its fulfillment in the external world.

Volition depends on knowledge: We desire what we know, not

what we don't know. Intention is essentially directional: It is aimed at an object which it hopes to attain. The satisfaction of the will depends on recognition of the attained as that which was sought. This voluntarist epistemology appears riddled with contradictions at every turn. It seems to postulate knowledge of the unknown, direction without destination, attainment of the already possessed. Granted that "from the infinity of real or possible objects, the judgment somehow picks out its own," [7] the operation by which it does so remains inherently puzzling. "But how," Royce asks, "how can you *mean,* how can you *aim at,* how can you *possess,* how can you *pick out,* how can you *identify,* what is not already present in essence to your own hidden self? Here is surely a deep question." [8]

Deep indeed. It provokes the further question of whether ideas ever do get outside the mind, of whether ideas ever can be objectively true. The whole problem, therefore, might be reduced to the problem of truth. Royce has a more interesting gambit to play: He reduces it to the problem of error.

He turns the difficulty inside out by arguing that if the object of the idea is what the idea intends, then the idea ought to be inerrant, since it knows what it wants. Error should be impossible. Since error is not impossible, since the failure of ideas to agree with objects is a part of experience, an inquiry into how this can be takes us back by another route into the theory that the internal meaning of ideas is decisive in knowledge. Error is not an oddity or a tragedy for Royce. It is "the steadfast rock on which we build." [9]

He begins with experience and reasons to the conditions implied by experience—which is to say that he remains a good Kantian in starting-point and method. His Kantian syllogism is before him as he starts his quest: If error is experienced as real, its conditions must be real; but error is experienced as real; ergo. Truth has been defined as agreement between idea and object. How is disagreement possible on voluntarist assumptions? What are the conditions that produce it?

Royce presents many examples of undoubted errors where their very existence is an embarrassment. Errors with regard to the past and the future seem to defy explanation since we cannot visit either section of the time-stream to find out whether a given judgment is erroneous or not. The knowledge of one man by another presents the difficulty in a striking way. How can John be mistaken about Thomas—when the only Thomas he knows is "his" Thomas, his mental conception of his friend, rather than the "real" Thomas? Shouldn't John be as sure about Thomas as if the latter were simply his mental construction? How is error possible in this case? "Common sense has said: 'Thomas never is in John's thought, and yet John can blunder about Thomas.' How shall we unravel this knot?" [10]

We unravel it by remarking that if Thomas could perceive John's thought about him, and since he obviously knows himself, *he* could tell if the thought was erroneous, if it missed its mark and by how much. Thomas, of course, cannot thus inspect both John's idea and himself to see if they agree; but if there is a third party who can, then to locate such a being would be to clear up the mystery.

Let us look at it this way. We have to explain "the partial knowledge that is sufficient to give the judgment its object, but insufficient to secure to the judgment its accuracy." [11] The theory has been propounded that an independent knower observing both thought and reality would be able to declare whether or not the idea has missed its object, whether the thinker has fallen into error. We have, fortunately, a common psychological experience to offer as an analogy of how this can actually happen. The memory often fails to grasp an idea that it possesses, and then it is correct to say that the individual *knows what he does not know*. He plays the part of an independent observer who knows that at which memory aims, and knows that it has failed to reach its object. He says to himself: "I *know* the name or the tune or the date, if only I could *remember* it." We have all had this experience of searching for what we know we know (fundamentally), and what we know we don't know (momentarily).

Royce takes this analogy and applies it to the problem of error. Just as faulty memory implies a person looking on and saying that it *is* faulty, so does faulty judgment imply a person performing the same function. Only, the epistemological question goes beyond a subjective division of finite faculties. Memory and its contents are within us, and, therefore, are explicable in terms of internal experience. Judgments about objective things are not explicable in the same terms. There is no use searching the mind for an extramental fact as we search the memory for a recollection.

To get back to John and Thomas, since the comparison has to be made, and since it is beyond human competence, there must be a superior intelligence to make it. The Absolute knows Thomas and also John's idea of Thomas. The Absolute is thus able to say how close John is to being right when he "aims" an idea at Thomas—just as an umpire says how close to the bull's-eye an archer has shot his arrow. The same argument covers the problem of time. The Absolute knows the entire time-stream at once—past, present, future—and so is able to declare how far ideas about the (to us, nonexistent) past and future are correct.

> What, then, is an error? An error, we reply is an incomplete thought that to a higher thought, which includes it and its intended object, is known as having failed in the purpose that it more or less clearly had, and that is fully realized in this higher thought. And without such higher inclusive thought, an assertion has no external object, and is no error.[12]

The operation of a "higher inclusive thought" is familiar to us. If I think that the dictionary is brown and find that it is red, I can correct my error because I hold in my mind at the same time the judgment that the dictionary is brown, the perception that it is red, and the conclusion that the perception proves the judgment to be erroneous. Corrigibility of any error is always carried out through a synthetic view, in a single mind, of the true and the false.

But even so commonplace an experience implies more than my limited intellect and sense perception: unless my thought and the dictionary both existed in a superior mind, I could not bend the one on the other. Royce here rephrases the argument that originated in the virtual self of Kant's transcendental unity of apperception and was developed into a real self by the post-Kantians from Fichte to Hegel. Royce's answer to the primary question of a voluntarist epistemology is this: "You can mean what your deeper self knows; you cannot mean what your deeper self doesn't know."[13]

This is the only explanation of how we get outside our own minds and reach objects. As participants in the Absolute, we know the truth; as subject to the limitations of the finite, we often miss the truth. We know (fundamentally) and we don't know (momentarily). That is why the internal meaning of ideas can be decisive in knowledge without ensuring infallibility.

The sum of errors about anything—and a fortiori about everything—is infinite. Since error is impossible without a mind to know it, infinite error involves the necessary existence of a being infinite in knowledge. Error implies omniscience. Internal meanings imply the Absolute.

III *The Theoretical Ought*

Royce having said that the external meaning of ideas is but an extension of the internal meaning, his conclusion is that we choose to have the world that surrounds us. Facts are stubborn because we want them to be.

This is another Roycean notion that seems bizarre. Does a person with a toothache really acknowledge its existence because he chooses to? Are the great tragedies and petty absurdities of life really a fulfillment of the purposes of those who are crushed or humiliated? The objects around us—do we *will* them to be there even when they foil our express desires? Would we not rather remove them, were it a matter of volition?

Royce replies to these queries with Fichte in mind—Fichte, the ethical idealist who held that I *demand* the world as I experience it in order to have the opportunity to do my duty therein. The Fichtean "I" is interpreted to mean that the absolute ego provides the material conditions through which the finite ego can struggle to victory and virtue. Royce takes the Fichtean principle and explains it in his own way. As to the two egos, he finds in his customary fashion that there is an analogy within the human psyche. If the absolute ego and the finite ego can conflict on the metaphysical level, so can lasting will and ephemeral wish on the psychological level.

An old idea in western thought, the antithesis of will and wish goes back at least to Plato and is prominent in modern thinkers like Rousseau and T. H. Green. A simple illustration suffices to make the point. Suppose a man is about to cross a bridge that, unknown to him, is in danger of collapsing. Others, who know the danger, seize him and pull him back. His momentary wish—

to step onto the bridge—is undoubtedly thwarted. But his fundamental will—not to endanger his life—is fulfilled. If he is a reasonable man, once the facts are explained to him he will agree that his real purpose was to be coerced: He *wanted* to be pushed away, and only his ignorance at the time prevented him from realizing it. He *willed* the stubborn facts that baffled him.

This psychology gives Royce evidence for his metaphysics of attention. We chafe at the constricting limits imposed on us by reality only because we do not see exactly how reality fulfills our deeper will. Our finitude causes our ignorance, and this in turn causes our lament about "stubborn facts" and "harsh reality." Actually, "What we experience is, in one aspect, always *our own will to be compelled by facts.*" [14]

Such is the theory by which Royce makes the external meaning of ideas an extension of the internal meaning without falling into solipsism, without making the universe mere illusion conjured up by the whims of the individual. The purpose (the intention, the plan of action) is everything, metaphysically speaking; and if we were the Absolute, we would understand the reason for saying so. As finite participants in the Absolute, we have to accept facts that appear beyond our purposes, mere external meanings that collide with our internal meanings. It is the nature of the finite will to seek for embodiment in objects and to cooperate in its own compulsion by those objects. As the man forced off the rickety bridge wanted to be so constrained, the will wants realities that are not changeable at will. "A fact, then, is at once that which my present will implies and presupposes, and that which, for this very reason, is in some aspect Other than what I find myself here and now producing, accomplishing, attaining." [15]

Objective things are acknowledged by the will; it consents to a belief in their actuality. But human beings notoriously differ with one another—and an individual with himself at different times—about the truly factual. Appearance conflicts with reality, illusion with truth. Why should we acknowledge reality and truth rather than appearance and illusion? Royce goes to Kant for an answer. The rational will, in Kantian ethics, is autonomous: It submits to a moral law that is imposed *by* itself *on* itself. To submit to a law imposed from without, whether theological or scientific in origin, would involve a heteronomy of the will, and would not be moral. This is Kant's practical ought. Royce the Fichtean considers the argument to be more widely applicable, and he makes truth as well as goodness derive from an autonomous will.

> When I say to myself, "Such and such deeds, not now done by me, would more fully express my will," my practical consciousness is the one which is summoned up by further saying, "Then I *ought* to tend, even now, towards such acts." And the theoretical *Ought* of our judgments about facts, like the practical *Ought* of Ethics, is after all definable in terms of what Kant called the Autonomy of the Will. I *ought* to do that which I even now, by implication, *mean to do*.[16]

I have internal meanings, and I ought to recognize as factual those objects that embody those internal meanings. I ought to acknowledge as real the ends at which my purposes are aimed. It is only rational to do so. If a man is dying of an incurable disease, here would seem to be a flat refutation of the thesis that reality ought to be acknowledged. Obviously the man doesn't *want* to be in so terrifying a condition. No, but fundamentally he *does* want the cosmos in which his deepest purposes are realized; and if that cosmos includes his affliction, then, despite all the apparent absurdity, he wants it too.

This is not fatalism. He may hope for a cure to be discovered in time to save him, and he may work for its discovery, for the cure may be part of reality. The essential thing is to be rational no matter what the cost, to acknowledge, so far as we have the insight, those stubborn facts that express our internal meanings coherently understood: "The facts, as real, are embodiments of my purpose, yet not of my purpose as just now it transiently seems, but as it ought to be viewed."[17] If a desperate man refuses to obey the theoretical ought, if he keeps thrusting unpleasant facts away from him, he invites lunacy. If a normal man refuses, he invites error. Each denies his own rationality.

Royce is thus an ethical idealist who is at the same time an absolute pragmatist. To know is to act; truth is to be found in what works; but what works, in the long run, always proves to be that which satisfies our purposes in an absolute sense. Roycean idealism, absolutism, and pragmatism come together in his assertion: "A judgment is not only a construction, but a resolve; not only a response but a precept. . . . It not only says: 'I believe'; it says, 'This is to be believed.' "[18]

Facts, according to Royce, are as intractably objective as the realists and pragmatists claim; they are acknowledged, and here the ethical idealists are right, for subjective reasons; and they are teleological, since they are the end toward which purposes strive. The theoretical ought explains both knowledge and reality by uniting the internal meaning and the external meaning of ideas.

IV *The Individual*

Royce has said that the idea, in seeking for the fulfillment of its internal meaning, strives to become ever more determinate until it reaches that which allows of no further determination. Ideas want to be embodied in individual realities.

Mere possibilities won't do. The possibility that there are ten ships in the harbor can be entertained as a passing fancy; but if the idea is serious, it longs to correspond to the actual number. Abstractions won't do either. The universal ship can be defined as an exercise in semantics; but the idea is in pursuit of real ships that really sail, really hold cargo, are really down there in the harbor. Look where we like, whether our interest be philosophy or politics or poetry or ping pong, our ideal is always to reach individuals. Science is no rebuttal to this assertion; for, if the theories of science are universal, they must eventually relate back to the things from which they are derived, and whose behavior they explain.

By this line of ratiocination, Royce arrives at the questions that pose a crux of his metaphysics: What is an individual? How do we know individuals? The first question is quickly answered. An individual is something unique, something that has no extant duplicate anywhere in the universe. This chair, this cat, this man—each is what it is to the exclusion of every other chair, cat, man. The idea, then, desires to be embodied in that which is unique.

But how do we reach such embodiment? How do we recognize an individual when we meet one? This question might seem to be trivial since we obviously are dealing with individuals all the time. Royce, however, has his reasons, following from his epistemology, for objecting to what he considers an over-simplified account of experience. When he runs down the cognitive faculties, he finds them all incapable of leading us to individuals. Reason being by definition the faculty that grasps universals, individuals clearly are outside its province, as the philosophers have generally noted. Reason puts us in touch with man rather than with this man—with the definable abstraction rather than with Socrates or Plato. The older thinkers tended to give the cognitive power in question to sense perception. Royce agrees that the senses do get closer to the basic reality, but he denies that they ever reach it. The eye, to take the most important sense, sees only patterns of color that "may indeed indicate individual beings; but they are not yet known as individuals." [19] The whiteness of Socrates is not unique, nor is his height or his shape or anything else that the eye takes in. Perhaps interpretation is the answer? No, for this intellectual operation falls as short as the others in attaining individuals. It may reveal other minds to us, but it never tells us that a given mind is unique.

Take a definite individual, Abraham Lincoln:

> The question might be raised at once, Is it possible, is it conceivable, that the world should contain another man who embodied just that now defined type—who looked, spoke, thought, felt, commanded, and succeeded as Lincoln the War President did? If you answer, "No"; then we may at once retort: How can you know that only one man of this or of any once defined type can exist? Have you the secret of creation? Is every man's mould shattered (to use the familiar metaphor) when the man is made? And if so, how come you to be aware of the fact?[20]

No appeal to the processes of cognition, whether on the intellectual or the sense level, whether singly or in combination, will lead us out of this metaphysical morass where individuals are indispensable to us and yet seem always to be beyond our grasp: "For what we find in our finite wanderings are always cases of types, instances of imperfectly fulfilled meanings." [21] "Individuality is something that we demand of our world, but that, in this present world of experience, we never find." [22]

Royce's conclusion is that individuality falls into "a category indefinable in purely theoretical terms." [23] Cognition having proved ineffectual when faced with the problem, there is no recourse but to the other side of human nature, to the volitional side. The will leads us directly to the individual. Love rather than thought or perception is responsible for our knowledge of the unique, and it has this power because it *makes* the unique instead of simply finding it as a matter of experience.

When cognition has presented an indeterminate conglomeration of universals (color, sound, texture, etc.), then the will intervenes to say that it intends to place a special value on this conglomeration. When a child becomes inconsolable over a broken toy, he so reacts not because there are no other toys like it, but because he places a unique value on *this* toy, and this one only. His mother places a unique value on *him* in the same way, albeit with a mature rather than a childish judgment. The people at the Capulet ball were but anonymous faces to Romeo until he singled out Juliet as the embodiment of his unique purpose. Thereafter he cannot believe that there is anyone comparable to her, and his will makes this to be a fact. She is for him an individual in the Roycean sense.

Since the individual is the reality we pursue, love is the key to being: "The problem of the lover is, therefore, to my mind, as technically metaphysical a problem as is that of any theologian. His 'exclusive interest' is a typical instance of the true principle of individuation."[24]

So far, according to Royce, so good. Still, we have reached what is only a half-way house on our path to a satisfactory solution. The search for a determinate embodiment of internal meaning is unending. No one ever reaches a complete determination in this life. A finite idea is never more than partially expressed by its object. Romeo will never know all that he would like to know about Juliet.

> Thus, in counting, the single numbers refer us further on in the number-series for the rest of what the counting process implies. If one merely counts the first ten numbers, there are still other numbers to count. A complete consciousness of the whole meaning of the number-series would complete this process of seeking Another by presenting the whole individual meaning of the number concept in a finished form.[25]

An idea, as Hegel has taught Royce, is always linked with others. We never do or can follow up more than a few of the relations implied in any instance, and finality escapes our finite faculties; but essentially no idea ever ceases to be a seeker: "As a fragment, my idea always looks elsewhere for the rest of itself." [26] Were we completely aware of our purposes, did we understand their full and final determination, we would know the totality of being. We would be one with the Absolute.

The concept of individuality is thus universally applicable. The will, impressing value and thereby creating uniqueness, operates in this world and beyond it. The Absolute is an individual as an object of self-love. This eternal love, projected downward into mundane things, makes both the universe and each of its contents unique individuals. We, as participants in the Absolute, choose from these divinely ordained individuals; we give those we prefer a value to the second degree, so to speak, so that they become individuals for us; the rest of the objects available to us remain either unknown or else clouded by a haze of abstraction and universality. "It is will, then, in God and in man, that logically determines the consciousness of individuality. The individual is, primarily, the object and expression of an exclusive interest, of a determinate selection." [27] In summation: "Individuality is a category of the satisfied Will." [28] These few words present the principle that is one of the central pillars of Royce's entire metaphysical system. "Schopenhauer," he observes, "Schopenhauer defines my world as my own will. If by my will he meant the individual embodiment and expression of the whole meaning of my ideas, he would thus be right." [29]

V *The Self*

The individual as such is the ultimate reality in Royce's metaphysics, but there is a subdivision of the class of individuals that has a significance beyond the rest. If all the things we know are ideas of the Absolute, some of these have ideas of their own; for they are sentient, cognitive, reflective beings. To the philosophy of the individual Royce adds the philosophy of the self.

The self, as Fichte has said, is a problem and not a principle. Like Fichte, Royce cannot reason in the manner of Descartes, for whom the existence of the self is the ultimate certainty from which the verities of epistemology and metaphysics may be deduced. Nor can Royce follow the empirical psychologists when they assume an elemental self and then describe a process whereby the infant "projects" himself into his environment and gradually achieves an experience of the not-self, the objective world.

As for the empirical self, Royce, reversing the customary belief, makes it derivative from social experience. The infant does not begin as a real person, but rather develops into such by contrast with the people and things that enter his area of sense perception. The eighteenth-century philosophers were fond of debating the character of a hypothetical human being who, separated from his parents at birth, might somehow have grown to adulthood without knowledge of other human beings. Royce's verdict is categorical: Whatever might be said of him, he could not be called truly a self. He would lack the self-consciousness that originates in "social contrast effects"—that develops as a child learns to imitate those around him.[30]

Here is the reason for the Roycean thesis that we would be virtually nothing without society and the state:

> In origin, then, the Empirical Ego is secondary to our social experience. In literal social life, the Ego is always known as in contrast to the Alter.[31]

> We have no habits of self-consciousness which are not derived from social habits, counterparts thereof. Where the analogy of our relations to our fellows ceases, reflection ceases also.[32]

> Play and conflict, rivalry and emulation, conscious imitation and conscious social contrasts between man and man—these are the sources of each man's consciousness about his own conduct.[33]

Self-development starts with the infant's learning to know himself from knowing others. Later, he learns from his interior life. His memory, imagination, and intellect come into play; and he realizes that the present condition of his ego can be changed with reference to its past, or that it can be improved upon through the perception of what it might be. The word "contrast" is operative. The self rises out of a social context and must constantly refer back to that context, no matter how reflectively adept anyone may become at the subjective building of his own character. Even the most mature person is compelled to consult others, for both action and thought depend on knowledge, and knowledge is a public thing, a matter of the individual self having the sense to understand that he must compare himself with the public self to see how far he is entertaining truth rather than illusion. "Practically," Royce argues, "I cannot be saved alone. Theoretically speaking, I cannot even find or define the truth in terms of my individual experience, without taking account of my relation to the community of those who know."[34]

Thus I do not recognize myself, and others afterward by analogy with myself. It is the impact of others that first teaches me what and who I am.

With this notion we are only a step away from a full Hegelian judgment on communal life. To the community, since we are essentially social beings, we owe practically all that we are. Under its nurturing influence we cease to be mere individuals in the sense that trees and cats are individuals: We become *human* individuals, persons, selves. We embody meaning and purpose as do all finite individuals, but, unlike the lower orders of existence, we are committed to cooperating with our meanings and purposes in the highest sense—that is, to making the best of ourselves. And this we can do only in the society of our fellow men, without whom we would be psychologically and morally reduced almost to the status of nonsentient individuals.

Royce, who sounds like an existentialist when he talks about the self making itself, sounds like a Marxist when he traces philosophical theories back to a social origin. Realism is the metaphysics of those who want entirely independent beings to exist because they are easier to deal with practically than the one being of the mystic or the validated beings of the critical rationalist. Realism is "the typical notion of socially respectable conservatism, whenever such conservatism begins to use the speech of technical philosophy."[35] The critical rationalists are more tied to liberalism because of the importance they place on value, credit, and hierarchies of moral, political, and social standing: "Very often they belong to what one might venture to call the left center of the parliament of thought—to the moderate Liberals of doctrinal discussion. . . ."[36] This is not Marxism because Royce does not make it a dogmatic universal principle. Had he been faced with a judgment on dialectical materialism, he would have seen at once its suicidal character, destroyed as it is from within by the same argument (economic determinism) that it brings against rival philosophies. Royce knew that other motives than social and economic bias are involved in philosophizing, and he certainly never regarded his absolute idealism as a crude mirror of a political position.

The empirical ego, to return to his argument, comes to self-consciousness through time, the time of physical and intellectual growth. The *nature* of the self, apart from its evolution, remains to be cleared up; and this can be done only by explaining its more intimate relation with time. What *is* the self? "Whatever the Self is, it is not a Thing. It is not, in Aristotle's or in Descartes' sense, a Substance." [37] "From this point of view [that of absolute idealism] the Self is not a Thing, but a Meaning embodied in a conscious life." [38]

Royce's point here is that he does not accept the reality of the soul, nor is he concerned with the traditional distinction between mind and matter. The true distinction in his philosophical psychology is between two kinds of meaning. The self corresponds to the not-self as does internal meaning to external meaning. The self has its purposes that seek fulfillment in objective things; it bows to the theoretical ought when it accepts the reality of those things; it is, therefore, an "Ethical Category" and "not a datum but an ideal." [39]

As an internal meaning, the self has a directional movement toward determinate embodiment; it traverses time. This puts us back in the middle of Royce's voluntaristic metaphysics. All individuals depend on will, but selves most of all; for they add to the teleology of the universe a teleology of their own: They can deliberately will their own ends. The connection with time is unbreakable.

> Time is the form of the Will; and the real world is a temporal world in so far as, in various regions of that world, seeking differs from attainment, pursuit is external to its own goal, the imperfect tends towards its own perfection, or in brief, the internal meanings of finite life gradually win, in successive stages, their union with their own external meaning.[40]

Now time in our experience, as Royce has already made abundantly clear, is a compound of the present and conceptual constructions from the past and future. We cannot confine ourselves to the present, which slips away even as we strive to prolong it. The stark instant is nothing. The specious present is all that we can know, and the specious present is not an instant but a segment of the time-stream. That is one reason why we cannot know the self by simply looking within. My present self will not stand still long enough to be inspected. It is necessarily integrated with my past and future selves. To solve the problem of the self calls for a profounder analysis than that of introspective psychology.

The momentary self has to be transcended in such a way that past, present, and future—while experienced as disparate because they lie in different sections of the time-stream—will at the same time become united for us when we survey them from the standpoint of a single purpose. The analogy that Royce uses here is that of music. The notes of a composition are played in succession, each holding a place in the temporal order that cannot be taken by a prior or subsequent note. All of the notes, nevertheless, must be unified and held together in the ear of the listener, or else the result will be a series of indiscriminate sounds rather than a melody. Try to imagine a Strauss waltz with the notes and chords spaced at ten-minute intervals, or all played at the same time. No, the *purpose* of the composer makes the music. And his purpose is not compromised, it is fulfilled, by the compulsion to conform to the laws of time.

The self, similarly, obeys time and masters it. When we look at succession discretely, we cannot escape the inexorable flow of past, present, and future. When we look at succession as a unified whole held together by purpose, plan, definition, then we break the time barrier and achieve a unity that is not diminished just because part of life is gone, and part has not yet come. As a melody does not lead up to a final note that makes the previous ones irrelevant, "the Self in its entirety is the whole of a self-representative or recurrent process, and not the mere last moment or stage of that process." [41]

The conclusion, however staggering it may seem, is forced on us: The self is infinite. Only apparently finite, it has the infinity of every self-representative system, of every system out of which infinity is generated by purpose. It is "strictly equal in infinity of structure and variety of content to the Absolute." [42] Since the human self thus appears to be neither finite nor identical with the Absolute, Royce prefers "to characterize the eternal ethical Individual as *infinite but partial*." [43]

The Absolute must be defined as infinite per se. We secondary infinites stand to this primal infinite as the even numbers to the whole number series, matching it in a one-to-one correspondence. We transcend the moment and know a segment of time in unity; the Absolute transcends time itself and knows all of its successions in unity. Time is eternity known bit-by-bit. Eternity is time known all at once. Relieved of our human limitations, we would enjoy the experience of the Absolute. Constrained by those limitations, the Absolute would be reduced to our experience. Our purposes, if completely embodied, would make us identical with the primal being.

In theological language, we are all parts of God, atoms of the divine essence. Is this pantheism, the identification of God with the world? Royce thinks that his mathematical analogy permits him an unqualified "no." The actual infinite in no way harms the independence of its parts; rather it posits their integrity as individuals. The even numbers retain their uniqueness after they have been put into a one-to-one correspondence with the whole numbers. Royce applies this same analysis to the relation of God and the world: We partake of divinity without being absorbed, as pantheism supposes, into the infinity of the Godhead. Our purposes are undoubtedly oriented toward complete fulfillment in the Absolute, but they remain now and forever *our* purposes.

Time, will, self, Absolute—each is a self-representative system joined to the others by the countless metaphysical relations. Unity pervades Royce's philosophy from top to bottom; so does pluralism.

The argument tells in favor of the immortality of the "infinite but partial self." The complete and final fulfillment implied by our vaguest passing whims, and more obviously by our deepest personal needs, can never be discovered in the world through which we pass from birth to death. The full determination of our internal meanings, our individuality, our selfhood, cannot be achieved except by direct union with the total actuality in which our human limitations will be removed. Internal meanings will then be immediately joined to external meanings, the secret of individual uniqueness will be revealed, the directional progress of the self across time will be satisfied by arrival at its eternal destination.

> In Eternity all is done, and we too rest from our labors. In Time there is no end to the individual ethical task.[44]

> And in the eternal world there are therefore moral personalities—individuals, who are yet one in God. The only immortality that I pretend to know about is precisely the presence of these individuals in the eternal world.[45]

VI *Facts and Values*

Royce has described individual selves working out their destiny through time toward eternity. What about the place where these moral dramas occur? How is the world to be understood? A cosmology must be developed since we know that theology and ethics do not explain the universe. At least in the obvious sense, whatever the deeper philosophical meanings, some things are non-moral as we meet them here and now. Common sense and science can both get along to a very large extent without recourse to metaphysical theory. Royce has to account for this fact. He has to explain, after the fashion of Kant, how moral behavior is possible in a world of law, mechanism, scientific uniformity.

Kant appeals to the two worlds of phenomena and noumena, the former rigidly controlled by scientific laws, the latter marked by freedom and ethical conduct. Royce appeals to the two worlds of description and appreciation. But for Royce it is actually a single world viewed from different perspectives. His is a double-aspect theory.

The world of description is the world interpreted in abstract terms that keep us from confounding truth and error. Truth is public; Royce repeats Peirce's dictum over and over. I may cherish illusions, dreams, fantasies, prejudices—until I test them against the opinions of my fellow men. If no one else can see what I think I see, then I ought to be reasonable enough to dismiss the experience as a quirk of my own making. The scientist whose experiments cannot be repeated in other laboratories is an imposter. Social universality is one criterion.

Temporal universality is another. I may compare my ideas, not with those of other people, but with those of my past self. The memory of the star that I saw last night can be invoked as a judge of the visual presence of the star tonight. The experience that affects me alone is the more strongly supported as true, the more it recurs. Of course I can still be mistaken just as the social consensus can be mistaken; but the general principle holds good that repetition is a guide to the truth; and the converse is unimpeachable: What cannot be universalized either socially or temporally remains suspect.

> Our finite life has its inner aspect in so far as it is just individual, the truth of our moments as such, the breaking of just our waves of consciousness on the beach. But our finite consciousness relates to outer and physical truth in so far as it *means* something that may be present for any and all intelligent moments and individuals.[46]

We attain this "outer and physical truth" by reproducing its conditions for the inspection of others or of ourselves. We reproduce the conditions by describing them. If I say that there really is a book on the table or a chemical reaction in the test tube, I must be able to describe the fact in such a way that anyone else in my place would be able to verify what I say.

I can do this because the experience is reproducible in abstract terms. Royce, echoing Kant's general thesis although not the specific Kantian analysis, attributes our descriptive power to the use of forms and categories of experience. The forms are space and time. The categories are quantity, quality, and so on. (Royce does not give a finished list of categories, as does Kant, because for him the categories are not deducible once and for all from the nature of our cognitive processes; the list continues to grow through the development of logic and science.) An instance of a Roycean descriptive statement is the one we have already formulated: "There is a brown dictionary on the table." No one can raise a problem of communication about *that* statement. Space, time, quantity, quality—all are pinpointed beyond ambiguity.

The world of description is therefore governed by natural law, necessity, regularity, repetition. It is supremely the world of science where reign the principle of causation, the uniformity of nature, the conservation of mass and energy. (Royce is speaking in terms of the science he knew, but his point could be restated in the light of relativity, quantum mechanics, and the mathematics of nuclear reaction. However scientific theories may change, science itself remains descriptive in the Roycean sense.)

Certitude, moreover, increases with describability. Mathematics being the most describable science, it is the most certain: "I know that all beings, if only they can count, must find that three and two make five. Perhaps the angels can't count; but if they can, this axiom is true for them. If I met an angel who declared that his experience had occasionally shown him a three and a two that did *not* make five, I should know at once what sort of an angel he was." [47]

It is easy to see why many scientists of Royce's time considered the world of description to be the only real world. It was the world they were dealing with in their laboratories, and they felt that it was self-sufficient. The crudest example of the belief came out in the form of scientific materialism, the theory that presumed to explain everything from stones to thoughts on the basis of atoms swirling through a Newtonian cosmos. The image was that of a machine moving under its own momentum, and the universe was called a self-winding watch.

Royce objected, not only because his idealist philosophy prompted him to, but also because he realized that science taken by itself contradicted the faith of the materialist. To say that knowledge is public is to say that description cannot describe itself, for public knowledge postulates communication—and communication is non-descriptive. The world of description is the world seen from the "outside." It looks quite different when seen from the "inside."

The universal describable aspect is paralleled by an aspect that is momentary, private, and indescribable without being illusory. This is the world of appreciation. It is the world of value judgments, of aesthetic reactions, of sensory feelings. It is the world of the toothache and the poignance that touches us in lyric poetry when the poet asks such a question as Villon's: "Where are the snows of yesteryear?" Appreciation and description are distinguished in a case like this:

> How my own hat feels when I pick it up, taking it from amongst a large number of hats in a dimly lighted cloak-room, is some-

> thing that I can only appreciate. I know my hat by the *feel* of it when I pick it up. *How* I know it I can't tell. On the other hand, that I find my hat hung on a peg higher than I myself left it, that it is hung on the right or the left side of the room, that just as I took it the clock struck ten, these are experiences that I pretend to be able to describe. I can tell you, so I say, just what I mean by them. I hold them to be experiences that anybody might have, whether he felt about my hat as I do, or did not.[48]

The evanescent feelings that slip away so quickly are just as real as the facts that can be reproduced at will. They are more fundamental because appreciations by themselves are possible, while descriptions cannot be made coherent without appreciations. When I appeal to some one else to corroborate a description, I do not appeal to his (describable) physics and physiology. I appeal to his (appreciable) mental character. I cannot perceive what goes on in his mind, nor can he give me descriptive knowledge of his thoughts, knowledge both public and universal. And yet it is precisely the communication between us, the intangible appreciative bond, that makes possible our common existence in the world of descriptions.

How communication occurs is part of Royce's absolutism. Appreciations become stable and lasting when mediated by the Absolute. Appreciable experiences are only part of our world, but the Absolute experiences everything, finite and infinite, as appreciable rather than descriptive. Yet once more it is our human limitations that constitute our stumbling-block. The world of description "is simply the way in which the world of appreciation, the world of the true and spiritual self, must needs appear when viewed by a finite being whose consciousness experiences in the forms of our space and of our time, and who is interested in giving to his fellows a dispassionate and universalized account of how he views it. Here is the permanent truth in Kant's doctrine."[49]

Were we liberated from those limitations, we would have direct access to the minds of one another, and then the world of description would vanish. We would experience nothing but a world of appreciation, "a world such as the organic Self in his wholeness might have present to him at a glance, or such as the community of conceived spiritual mind-readers might share.

It would be a world whose Universals were of the type that Hegel defined." [50]

It would be governed by the categories of self-consciousness instead of the abstract categories—purpose and value replacing scientific laws. It would be a world in which determinism would give way to history—the fulfillment of purpose through time replacing the cosmic machine that has no destiny.

So much we can infer. The actual experience must wait until we reach the next world. In our present state, the one world both controls us imperiously by its laws, and submits to our free exercise of our sensitive, emotional, rational selfhood. "To live in time by virtue of one's physical nature, but out of time by virtue of one's very consciousness of time itself, is to share in the eternal freedom, and to be a moral agent." [51]

We live in a world of facts and values.

VII *Loyalty to Loyalty*

The values of highest import are moral values. The distinction between good and evil, between right and wrong, colors Royce's whole interpretation of the universe as it does that of any moralist; but it means more to him than to most since he cleaves consistently to the ethical idealism that he learned from Fichte. He balances knowledge and conduct in a manner that descends ultimately from Kant, from the *Critique of Pure Reason* supplemented by the *Critique of Practical Reason,* and is elaborated in the works of the post-Kantian idealists. Knowledge is a matter of the theoretical ought by which we acknowledge the facts that we *should* acknowledge; and the denial of the theoretical ought pushes us into irrationality and error. Conduct is a matter of the practical ought by which we acknowledge our duty and perform the acts that we *should* perform; and the denial of the practical ought pushes us into irrationality and sin.

Royce is thus a philosopher for whom ethics begins with metaphysics. Some of the ideas that allow him to shift easily from the one sphere to the other are woven together in this salient passage:

> *One* is the Absolute, because in *mere* multiplicity there would

> be no finality of insight. *Many* is the Absolute, because in the interrelationships of contrasted expressions of a single Will lies the only opportunity for the embodiment of wholeness of life, and for the possession of Self-consciousness by the Absolute. . . . *Individuals* are all the various expressions of the Absolute, in so far as they are Many; just because, where the One is an individual, every aspect and element of its self-expression is unique. *Free,* in its own degree, is every individual will amongst all the wills that the world-life expresses because every such will, as unique, is in some respect underivable from the others. *Temporal* is the world order, because, so far as we can know, time is the universal form of the expression of Will. *Eternal* is this same world order, because past, present and future time equally belong to the Real, and their Being implies, by definition, that they are present, in their wholeness, to the final insight.[52]

Another pair of terms apply to the finite world—the terms "good" and "evil." Royce, who attacks the problem of evil first from the standpoint of metaphysical reality, argues that existence as we know it curtails the amount of good that is possible in the universe. Nothing short of the Absolute can be perfect. Since the human will is always questing for something, always looking for determinate objective embodiment, always bent on the unattainable fulfillment of its meanings—therefore it suffers lack by its very nature. This metaphysical evil is necessary. Our duty is to accept that without which we could not be, and to feel grateful for the chance to struggle with the harsh temporal conditions of virtue and salvation. Endurance, to mention one virtue, would be nothing without something to endure.

The second kind of evil is natural evil. Some defects that offend our ethical sense are merely empirical, brute happenings without rhyme or reason to our limited intelligence. Illness, death, fire, flood—these follow, not from the metaphysics of finitude, but from scientific laws that could be other than they are. This is the evil that men find so puzzling. This is the problem of Job.

Royce, it goes without saying, does not claim to have an explanation of natural evil. But he *does* claim to make it more understandable by placing it in the context of his absolutism. Evil exists to be overcome. The individual triumphs through suffering. The Absolute, who, be it remembered, is one with the individual, also triumphs through suffering. The difference is that the Absolute knows good as well as truth in perfect unity, while we have to act by partial insights and enveloped in profound mystery.

> The only way to give our view of Being rationality is to see that we long for the Absolute only in so far as in us the Absolute also longs, and seeks, through our very temporal striving, the peace that is nowhere in Time, but only, and yet absolutely, in Eternity. Were there then no longing in Time, there would be no peace in Eternity.[53]
>
> . . . .
>
> The answer to Job is: God is not in ultimate essence another being than yourself. He is the Absolute Being. You truly are one with God, part of his life. He is the very soul of your soul. And so, here is the first truth: When you suffer, *your sufferings are God's sufferings,* not his external work, not his external penalty, not the fruit of his neglect, but identically his own personal woe.[54]

Why should divinity itself suffer? For the same reason that we do, namely, that suffering is an indispensable condition of goodness and right. Our duty is to alleviate natural evil all we can, to accept what we cannot alleviate, and to solace ourselves with the reminder that our suffering is ennobled by the transcendent truth that God shares it with us. "The eternal world contains Gethsemane." [55]

The third kind of evil is human evil—sin, iniquity, the deliberate violation of the moral law. How does sin arise in free men whose essential purposes all point to union with the Absolute, and therefore to virtue? Royce returns to his theory of attention. Finitude as such is beset with *involuntary inattention,* the inability to keep an eye on everything in the universe. Free finitude is prone to *voluntary inattention,* the desire not to know everything about a given moral situation.

> To attend, is to be at once guided in your momentary deed by what you know, and determined in your knowledge by what you do. And, as Professor James has so successfully pointed out, and as we ourselves have maintained from the outset of the present series, the central feature of every voluntary deed, the constitutive principle of every finite life, is a process of attention.[56]

The man who meditates embezzlement may turn his thought into reality if he focuses his attention squarely on what he hopes to gain. He may stay his hand if he broadens his attention and considers all the factors—his duty to others, his personal integrity, the possibility of being caught, and so on. Attention is a reliable clue to personality: "As a man attends, so is he, so he knows, and so too, he acts, or voluntarily refrains from action."[57]

Sin does not escape the net of Royce's absolutism. Anger, greed, envy, pride, dishonesty, concupiscence—all afford us the opportunity to conquer them in the name of virtue. We can *use* them to our profit. In the same way does the Absolute *use* the sins that men do not conquer, that they either reluctantly or willingly traffic with. "In God, so we say to the willful sinner, you are part of a good will, which bears just such organic relation to your sinfulness as, in a good man, his virtue bears to the evil impulse that forms a part of his goodness."[58] Absolute: Sin::Saint:Temptation.

The finite self *needs* temptation. The absolute self *needs* sin. Our duty is to resist sin in ourselves, and in others as far as we can, without supposing that its temporal victories in any sense affront the dictum of Leibniz that this is "the best of possible worlds."[59]

The strange thing about sin is that, while intensely personal and attributable only to the individual sinner, it functions as a bond between human beings. Since we are all committed to the fulfillment of purposes that are both ours and the Absolute's, no one can be indifferent to the violation of those purposes. Royce, again sounding like an existentialist before his time, connects everything in the moral world with everything else through strands of metaphysical meaning, so that to tamper with one node is to shake the whole web.

> And thus the significance of my moral existence, however petty my apparent range of influence, and however limited in one sense my powers may be, extends, in another sense, without limit, through the whole range of the future temporal order. In brief, it is with your moral efficacy as with your physical efficacy when viewed in accordance with the ideal theory of gravitation. According to that theory, when you move, you move, however little, the whole earth and the sun and the stars.[60]

There is a solidarity of the moral order between man and God, and between man and man. The sin of one man is the sin of all, primarily of the sinner, but secondarily touching all humanity to some degree.

Evil, then, following Hegel, is the material of virtue. Our duty is to be virtuous. But what does this mean in practice? How am I to distinguish right from wrong in the immensely complicated moral dilemmas of everyday life?

Royce offers as a criterion his philosophy of loyalty. It would be more accurate to say *the* criterion inasmuch as he thinks that the virtue of loyalty actually embraces all the virtues: "In loyalty, when loyalty is properly defined, is the fulfillment of the whole moral law." [61] The proper definition of loyalty is "the practically devoted love of an individual for a community," [62] or "the willing and practical and thoroughgoing devotion of a person to a cause." [63]

The patriot who defends his country, the martyr who sacrifices himself for his faith, the captain who makes sure of being the last to leave his sinking ship—that types such as these are loyal needs no laboring. Even a virtue like veracity, however, comes under the Roycean definition, for veracity is loyalty to the cause of truth; and it has the beneficial social effect of encouraging veracity in others.

What about the times when loyalties conflict? What is the patriot to do when he considers the fact that there are patriots on the enemy side? Royce's exhortation is to do what promises to produce the greatest amount of loyalty in the world: Be loyal to loyalty. He thought that he was giving a practical example of his precept during World War I when he attacked the Germans as foes of loyalty—*their* loyalty being destructive of so many other loyalties.

By so doing he actually gave an example of another of his principles. Suppose one makes a mistake? It is conceivable that Royce might have lived to admit that he made a mistake in 1916, and he could have defended himself on the ground that he never claimed omniscience for the practitioners of loyalty. The best that anyone can do is to weigh the evidence before him, strike a balance, and then act as energetically as if he were sure of being right: "We are fallible, but we can be decisive and faithful; and this is loyalty." [64]

Royce tries to make his theory concrete by integrating free volition with intuition, instinct, and custom. Some loyalties are rightly honored because our feelings support them; others, because of the laws and mores of our society. These need only to be infused with rational intention to make the rounded moral personality, for "Loyalty is a perfect synthesis of certain natural desires, of some range of social conformity, and of your own deliberate choice."[65] To lead a virtuous life, take all three into account—and be loyal to loyalty.

VIII *The Christian Religion*

There is, according to Royce, a species of loyalty to a particular community that opens to man a path to the highest possible virtue. An active and practical commitment to Christianity brings with it the most comprehensive system of loyalties, centered as this religion is on the good of man, capable as it is of persuading men to accept its faith, fortifying them as it does in their resolve to act in the light of faith.

So much of a preface to religion sounds as if Royce is about to launch into a technical analysis of the great Christian ideas after the fashion of the theologians. The reader expects the usual list of headings: Christologies, creeds, dogmas, church history, heresies, schisms. This, however, and despite his two substantial tomes called *The Problem of Christianity,* is not Royce's intention. He does not deal with theology in any comprehensive way. He leaves to one side such basic Christian mysteries as the Trinity, the Incarnation, and the Sacraments. He even leaves untouched the psychology of religious mysticism, the direct inspiration that moved the great mystics from St. Paul to St. Teresa.

What kind of a theologian, then, is Josiah Royce? He is the direct antithesis of William James. In *The Varieties of Religious Experience,* James investigates highly personalized religion rather than corporate forms of worship. He is fascinated by the mystical or occult experiences of individuals—Bunyan, Tolstoi, Madame Blavatsky. He remains the individualist, the pragmatist, the radical empiricist, for whom churches and ecclesiastical systems are "conventional" and therefore irrelevant. Royce, the metaphysical idealist and philosopher of the community, the thinker for whom all meaningful experience must be communal, finds that James has tumbled into "a profound and momentous error." [66] Religion for Royce gets its worth from common rather than from individual experience, or, taking it the other way around, the individual experience of consequence is that which manifests itself in the life of a religious community.

Royce asks: "In what sense can the modern man consistently be, in creed, a Christian?" [67] To find an acceptable answer to this question he takes up the three problems of the church, original sin, and redemption.

The church begins with the teaching of Christ that God is Love, that this divine love radiates through the world, and that each man should in turn love not only God but his fellow men. The Apostle to the Gentiles gives the doctrine of Christ an institutionalized form by relating the psychology of love to the community of believers: "In sum, Christian love, as Paul conceives it, takes the form of loyalty. This is Paul's simple but vast transformation of Christian love." [68] The church embodies the Christian form of loyalty. If and when the church becomes a universal community of all mankind, then loyalty to loyalty will have reached the ultimate of which men are ethically and religiously capable.

The Christian revelation and the Christian church are necessary because all men are sinners who cannot by themselves conquer their sin. Royce seeks to make this Pauline doctrine persuasive by interpreting it in terms of social empiricism. As we look about us, we see that individuals and society necessarily conflict, no matter how much each may need the other. The individual insists on expressing his personality in actions that often are asocial; society often baffles his legitimate interests with its customs and laws; and even the best relations between them cannot prevent animosities from arising. The tension is in direct ratio of one to the other as they develop. The highest cultures produce the most dangerous rebels—witness the history of the Greeks and the Jews. These empirical facts are so profound for Royce that he sees in them the explanation of original sin: "Man's fallen state is due to his nature as a social animal." [69]

St. Paul's moral theology is not just an abstract or mystical appeal to faith. Original sin is not an invention of the theologians. It is the hardest of the hard facts that we face as ethical beings. It it the penalty for being what we are—free finite selves forced by our very nature to live together.

Christianity solves the problem of sin by the principle of grace. Royce accepts this, expresses it in his particular phraseology, and uses it for explanatory purposes on the temporal as well as the eternal level: "The problem of grace is the problem of the origin of loyalty; and is again a perfectly human problem."[70] There is a kind of natural loyalty that Royce has already described, the kind that inspires the patriot. We know from experience that we must have a higher form of loyalty to counteract original sin. This loyalty is the grace of God; and the church that Christ founded is a well-spring of grace among men.

But it is not enough that a good man should have established a good community for the dissemination of a good moral code. Redemption is indispensable. In its most evident manifestation, redemption does not necessitate a supernatural explanation. As there are communities apart from the community of the Christian church, as loyalty can flourish among men short of Christian grace, just so is there a natural redemption that operates without relation to Christian redemption. The criminal, the traitor who offends society, can be redeemed by society. Through punishment, correction, and remorse he can be turned into a loyal citizen. "I insist that our problem is as familiar and empirical as is death or grief."[71]

Royce refers to three qualities that any atonement must have. It must involve a good deed that could not have been done without the evil deed. It must leave the world better than before. It must be the work of a representative of the community. We find all three in natural atonement. We find all three raised to transcendent mystery in the supernatural Atonement to which the Christian church is a living witness.

> And this atoning work of Christ was for Christian feeling a deed that was made possible only through man's sin, but that somehow was so wise and so rich and so beautiful and divinely fair that, after this work was done, the world was a better world than it would have been had *man* never sinned.[72]

Royce deliberately refuses to discuss the exact meaning of the Atonement—whether Christ cancelled the sin of Adam by satisfying the offended majesty of God (the penal theory) or by offering to man a model of grace and sinlessness (the moral theory). It is enough for Royce that men are now able to see why they should be loyal to the community of the church—and to *be* loyal.

Nor does Royce expend much time or thought on the theology of faith. Loyalty is still enough to give him the theological principle he needs: "Let your Christology be the practical acknowledgment of the Spirit of the Universal and Beloved Community. This is the sufficient and practical faith." [73]

Royce's concept of Christianity in theory and practice comes down to a one-sentence summary: "The thesis of this book is that the essence of Christianity, as the Apostle Paul stated that essence, depends upon regarding the being which the early Christian Church believed itself to represent, and the being which I call, in this book, the 'Beloved Community,' as the true source, through loyalty, of the salvation of man." [74]

Royce's metaphysics defines both self and society as communities in which the process of interpretation unifies the temporal sequence of past, present, and future into a single organism. The argument applies pre-eminently to the Christian church and its Founder: "I stand for the importance of this process which has led Christianity to regard a community not merely as an aggregate but as a Person, and at the same time to enrich its ideal memory of a Person until he became transformed into a Community." [75] The Roycean version of Christianity follows substantially from the principles of Roycean metaphysics.

XI *Some Objections to Royce*

Royce considered his type of philosophy "a sure possession of human thought," [76] but most philosophers of his time and ours have declined to accept it as such. Those who approach the problems of life and mind from the standpoint of other systems—realism, pragmatism, materialism, analysis, logical positivism, etc.—reject absolute idealism as a matter of course. Apart from general theory, vigorous dissenting opinions have been registered to particular elements of Royce's thought. Some of these have already been mentioned in earlier pages of this book. Many others could be adduced since Royce has been challenged on every subject of this chapter. Probably everyone who examines his philosophy with care will come away from it troubled by reservations. One may feel that the relation of absolute mind and human mind is an enigma rather than an explanation; or that the senses *do* discover individuals; or that the self precedes society instead of being derived from it; or that Royce's Christianity is rather tepid because of his failure to pay enough attention to Christology, mystical theology, and the history of the church.

To analyze fully the corpus of Royce criticism would require at least another volume. What follows here is a brief indication of the most serious negative criticism that has been brought against the Roycean system—criticism of its absolutism, its voluntarism, and its ethics.

Absolutism. From the moment that the post-Kantian idealists began transforming Kant's virtual self into a real self, there were those who shuddered at the result. When Royce began to reformulate post-Kantian thought, he too provoked shudders.

His critics, for all his protests and his appeals to logical and mathematical analogies, refused to admit that he had safeguarded pluralism either metaphysically or ethically. He remained for them a monist. They accused him of describing the "block universe" that James disliked so much. They argued that the Absolute swallowed up everything else, if Royce's theory were true. They argued that this was pantheism, the identification of God with the world, leaving no room for human freedom. They argued that Royce in one place or another attributes both human frailities to the Absolute (James) and absolute power to human beings (Santayana)—in short that he unites God and man "with a literalness truly appalling" (Howison).[77]

As to how Royce managed to think himself into so impossible a position, it has been alleged that he confuses truth with reality (Mackintosh), that he confuses truth with veracity (Perry), and more generally that he confuses logical being with real being (Tallon).[78]

Voluntarism. That intellect and will go together is almost a cliché in psychology. The philosophical psychologists, probing the thought processes with their conceptual techniques, are unable to see how an idea could exist without an accompanying volition, or vice versa. The experimental psychologists have been unable to locate a divorce of the two faculties in their laboratories. Ideas involve attitudes. To that extent Royce is vindicated.

But his specific interpretation has attracted no such consensus of favorable opinion. The dominance of internal meaning over external meaning has been attacked because the selection of an object does not determine its content (Ewing); because the relation of idea to object is not that of purpose to fulfillment (Rogers); because finite fulfillment makes the purpose dominant while the absolute system of ideas gives supremacy to the object (Moore); because, if the internal meaning is as basic as Royce says, then no distinction remains between fact and fantasy (Cunningham).[79] Even a thinker very favorable to Royce's type of philosophizing (Hocking) holds that Royce, after properly asserting that facts are real for us because we acknowledge them, misses the correlative truth that facts are more than the fulfillment of our purposes, and reality more than the complete fulfillment of our purposes.[80]

Ethics. Royce's moral philosophy has been impugned for many reasons, most of which reduce to a denial of his theory of good and evil, or a denial of his criterion for distinguishing between right and wrong.

That evil exists so that we may overcome it, or at least so that we may struggle through to virtue even when the cause is lost, and that the suffering of the Absolute answers the problem of Job—all this seems obviously unsound to some readers of Royce. Does goodness really imply evil, and are there no virtues (like Pauline charity) that can exist without temptation? If everything that happens in the world, good and evil alike, redounds to the glory of the Absolute, is our struggle to be virtuous anything more than a puppet drama without moral or religious significance? Since the Absolute triumphs over finite evil, can Royce claim without self-contradiction that the Absolute suffers as we often-defeated mortals do? Can ignorance be denied, while suffering is asserted, of the Absolute? Each of these questions has drawn a negative reply (Cronin, Milne, Jefferson, Hartshorne).[81]

Even granted the correctness of Royce's theory of evil, we still might demur at the moral criterion by which he proposes to guide us to the side of goodness and right. His principle of loyalty to loyalty may be too abstract to be of practical use amid the confusion of daily conduct (Everett); loyalty to the ideal community may conflict with loyalty to a real community (Werkmeister); indeed, loyalty as a precept for human beings may contribute to hostility between communities (Perry).[82]

Negative criticism of Royce is more in evidence today than at any time since his death—but so is positive criticism. Both sides agree on this at least, that his philosophy is one of the perdurable systems. The philosophers of our time are almost obligated to master the system, and then either to defend it or to attack it. Indifference is becoming as difficult as it was when William James found that his integrity demanded an intellectual showdown with Josiah Royce.

CHAPTER 5

The Relevance of Royce

PHILOSOPHY is a special thing among the intellectual disciplines. With literature or history or (above all) mathematics, there is a well-defined area containing an accepted body of knowledge such that most professionals are at one in their most important judgments. No one asks whether analytical geometry is a science; or whether Shakespeare is worth reading; or whether Napoleon is a commanding figure in modern European history.

Dissent arises at the point where philosophy crosses a subject. Aesthetics, historicism, mathematicism—each of these is an arena for warring factions. The parent of them all, metaphysics, seems simply anarchic. Not only do the various schools and systems contend, but there is no consensus among philosophers as to the content or aim of metaphysics, while some go so far as to deny its right to exist. Idealists can barely communicate with analysts, or materialists with Thomists. Hence the ease with which the unphilosophical slip into scepticism and doubt about all the philosophies.

Yet, scepticism itself is a philosophy: As Aristotle says, if you defend philosophy you philosophize, and if you attack philosophy you philosophize. The question is not whether you will have philosophy, but what kind of philosophy you will have. Your choice could have been worse if, after canvassing the alternatives, you settle on the absolute idealism of Josiah Royce. Not only is his system a "living option," to requote William James, but it presents an abundance of theses for further development. His principles could be extended almost indefinitely, and used by thinkers of originality to solve problems that have emerged since his death. We could have Roycean verdicts on logical positivism, on the fourth dimension, on the ethics of nuclear war, on Christian unity.

Some of this is already part of contemporary philosophy. Royce has been a harbinger of, or a direct influence on, outstanding philosophers at home and abroad. He is mentioned as a contributor to modern logic by Russell and Lewis. His metaphysics helped to fashion the existentialism of Marcel. His philosophy of the community is like that of Buber, his dialectical theology like that of Barth, Niebuhr and Hocking. He has a place in the metaphysics of personalism. The list could be lengthened, and time will lengthen it further.

Without becoming that technical, and even if we find Royce's system unacceptable, there are subsidiary reasons for making ourselves acquainted with his philosophy. One doesn't have to be a Platonist to appreciate Plato, or a Thomist to appreciate Aquinas—or a Roycean to appreciate Royce. James thought Royce the most plausible proponent of absolute idealism, and absolute idealism is a philosophy of which every educated person should know something. Marcel said that Royce is an indispensable part of modern philosophical thought, so that to be unfamiliar with him constitutes a distinct gap in one's awareness of the intellectual milieu. Even the controversy about Royce's metaphysical system reveals his relevance. His main opponents have been great opponents: James, Howison, Dewey, Perry. He has had great defenders: Marcel, Hocking. To follow this controversy is a lesson in the clarification of great ideas.

As historian of ideas, Royce is a guide to his period. He informs us of what was going on in Germany and America. He explains how James and Peirce extended American thought; he is the best witness to his own part in its extension. With his works in hand, we can see more clearly how and why the naïve era of Fiske and Wright gave way to the disciplined era of Dewey, Santayana, and Whitehead.

There is an intellectual exercise through which every student of philosophy should be put at least once, the exercise of mastering a complex system made up of many elements bound together by a few powerful guiding theories. Royce, on a par with, say, Plotinus, Wolf, Malebranche and Mill, is a good candidate for this rigorous treatment right after the supreme masters like

Aristotle and Kant. He may be America's best philosopher. Although he himself awarded pride of place to Edwards, Emerson, and James, we at this distance can see that Emerson has to be dropped: His transcendentalism is too inexact to be convincing or rewarding. James doesn't belong in the triad either. He didn't break trail for subsequent thinkers as did Royce in so many ways; he didn't leave the most puzzling defense of a profound and false metaphysical notion as did Edwards (on the bondage of the will). James was a more imposing personality than any other American who has taken to philosophy, and one of our really great men. But the three foremost American philosophers, to my mind, are Peirce, Royce, and Edwards, in that order.

What has Royce to offer the general reading public? He offers "philosophy for the layman." No one else writing in English, perhaps no one since Plato, has made so much accurate information about difficult philosophical theories so palatable to the uninitiated. Dozens of pages of *The Spirit of Modern Philosophy* are as entertaining as a novel.

On the practical level, Royce is an enduring diagnostician of the American psyche. He has something of interest to say on education, race relations, the ethics of labor and management, and states rights versus the federal government. He identifies factors that lie behind the existing national malaise, although his prescriptions may not be potent enough for America in the latter half of the twentieth century.

He speaks to Americans today partly because his advice is anchored to their historical past; but this is not the only reason for reading his historical works. Sociological prepossessions are unnecessary. He writes history as it should be written—with feeling, judgment, and style. His *California* is not unworthy of standing on the shelf beside *The Oregon Trail* and *The Conquest of Mexico*.

Royce's literary criticism needs more study. No mere tail to his philosophical kite, it makes him an exemplar of one type of critic, the type that shuns pure literary values for the values that are precipitated by the union of ideas and emotions when expressed in words. Fine monographs could exploit the material in his critical writings: Royce on Goethe, Royce on Browning as Philosopher, Royce on the Romantic Movement.

Then, Royce is a maker of literature. If no one would call *The Feud of Oakfield Creek* an important novel in its own right, there remains to lend it a unique interest the background against which it was produced—the background compounded of the metaphysician-turned-novelist, romantic California, erudite Harvard, and the piquant presence of William James. Royce has this in common with Henry Adams, that his novel takes on an added dimension when the reader bears in mind who, what, and where the novelist was.

Royce should be famous for his achievements in half-a-dozen fields. He suffers from a contracted reputation because he is read piecemeal rather than comprehensively. This might not matter, except that the same items of his bibliography, the philosophical items, overshadow the rest. His true stature cannot be discerned unless he is read systematically from *The World and the Individual* to *The Feud of Oakfield Creek*, from "Joseph Le Conte" to "The Implications of Self-consciousness," from "The Problem of Paracelsus" to *The Problem of Christianity*.

Josiah Royce is one of the most versatile minds in the history of American thought. He writes as a man of broad and humane culture. He should be read primarily because reading him is a liberal education.

Notes and References

Chapter One

1. William James, *Selected Papers on Philosophy,* Everyman edition (London, 1917), p. 9. The passage is an abridgment of *The Religious Aspect of Philosophy* (New York, 1885), pp. 160-62.
2. *In the Spirit of William James* (New Haven, Conn., 1938), p. 41.
3. *Fugitive Essays,* ed. by J. Loewenberg (Cambridge, Mass., 1920), p. 4.
4. *Ibid.*
5. *Ibid.*, p. 91.
6. *Ibid.*, p. 262.
7. *The Spirit of Modern Philosophy* (Boston, 1892), pp. 109-10.
8. *Ibid.*, p. 159.
9. *The World and the Individual,* I (New York, 1899), 423.
10. *The World and the Individual,* II (New York, 1901), 201-2.
11. *The Spirit of Modern Philosophy,* p. 2.
12. *The Problem of Christianity* (New York, 1913), I, 120.
13. "Pessimism and Modern Thought," *Fugitive Essays,* p. 176.
14. *The Conception of God* (New York, 1897), p. 15.
15. *The World and the Individual,* I. 381.
16. *Ibid.*, p. 48.
17. "Shelley and the Revolution," *Fugitive Essays,* p. 76.
18. "Joseph Le Conte," *International Monthly,* IV (1901), 334.
19. *Contemporary Idealism in America,* ed. by Clifford Barrett (New York, 1932), p. 5; *The Development of Harvard University since the Inauguration of President Eliot,* ed. by Samuel Eliot Morison (Cambridge, Mass., 1930), p. 11.
20. Ralph Barton Perry, *The Thought and Character of William James,* I (Boston, 1935), 810.
21. "Shelley and the Revolution," p. 93.
22. *Ibid.*, p. 82.
23. "Tennyson and Pessimism," *Studies in Good and Evil* (New York, 1906), p. 77.
24. "Shelley and the Revolution," p. 70.
25. *The Spirit of Modern Philosophy,* p. 226.
26. *Fugitive Essays,* pp. 9-10.

27. Section II of "Pessimism and Modern Thought" reappears as Chapter V of *The Religious Aspect of Philosophy.*

28. "Autobiographical Sketch: Words of Professor Royce at the Walton Hotel at Philadelphia, December 29, 1915," *The Hope of the Great Community* (New York, 1916), p. 129.

29. *Fugitive Essays,* p. 29.

30. "Pessimism and Modern Thought," p. 161.

31. "Schiller's Ethical Studies," *Fugitive Essays,* p. 42.

32. "Pessimism and Modern Thought," p. 170.

33. "Tennyson and Pessimism," p. 87.

34. "Pessimism and Modern Thought," p. 166.

35. *Ibid.,* p. 162.

36. *The Religious Aspect of Philosophy,* p. 118.

37. "The Decay of Earnestness," *Fugitive Essays,* p. 311.

38. *The Spirit of Modern Philosophy,* p. 166.

39. "The Problem of Paracelsus," *Fugitive Essays,* p. 407.

40. *The Spirit of Modern Philosophy,* pp. 226-27.

41. *California from the Conquest in 1846 to the Second Vigilance Committee in San Francisco: A Study of American Character* (New York, 1948), p. 394.

42. *Ibid.,* p. 40.

43. *Ibid.,* p. 41.

44. *Ibid.,* p. 61.

45. *Ibid.,* p. 32.

46. *Ibid.,* pp. 50-51.

47. *Ibid.,* p. 144.

48. *Ibid.,* p. 117.

49. He pursues his argument through no less than seventy-five pages of *California* in the chapter called "The American as Conqueror: The Secret Mission and the Bear Flag," pp. 43-118. The anti-Frémont thesis is the subject of his articles "Frémont," *Atlantic Monthly,* LXVI (1890), 548-57; "The Frémont Legend," *The Nation,* LII (1891), 423-25; "Montgomery and Frémont: New Documents on the Bear Flag Affair," *The Century Magazine,* XLI (1891), 780-83. The most prominent latter-day defender of Frémont is Alan Nevins, who accepts Frémont's explanation to Royce, and credits him with being the best kind of military man, the kind who knows when the situation demands that he act at once, and energetically. See *Frémont, Pathmaker of the West* (New York, 1939), pp. 244, 282-83, 608-9. Royce is supported by Robert Glass Cleland in the 1948 reprint of *California,* introduction, p. xvii.

50. *California,* p. 97.

51. *Ibid.,* p. 117.

52. *Ibid.,* p. 218.

53. *Ibid.*, p. 281.
54. *Ibid.*, p. 371.
55. *Ibid.*, p. 296.
56. *The Philosophy of Loyalty* (New York, 1908), p. 243.
57. *Character and Opinion in the United States* (New York, 1920), p. 85.
58. *The Feud of Oakfield Creek: A Novel of California Life* (New York, 1887), p. 137.
59. *Ibid.*, p. 290.
60. *The World and the Individual*, II, 124.
61. *The Feud of Oakfield Creek*, p. 160.
62. *Ibid.*, p. 274.
63. *Ibid.*, pp. 436-37.
64. *Ibid.*, p. 203.
65. *Ibid.*, p. 197.
66. *Ibid.*, p. 166.
67. *Ibid.*, pp. 232-33.

Chapter Two

1. *Fugitive Essays*, p. 6.
2. "Autobiographical Sketch," *The Hope of the Great Community*, pp. 122-23.
3. A remarkable example of her bravery on the trail is her encounter with a coyote, *A Frontier Lady: Recollections of the Gold Rush and Early California*, ed. by Ralph Henry Gabriel (New Haven, Conn., 1923), p. 48. Royce drew on her memories of the trek West in *California*, pp. 190-94.
4. *A Frontier Lady*, pp. 79-140, *passim; California*, pp. 319-20.
5. "Autobiographical Sketch," pp. 123-24.
6. *Ibid.*, p. 128.
7. "Joseph Le Conte," p. 329.
8. *The Conception of God*, p. 4.
9. *Ibid.*, pp. 77-78.
10. *Ibid.*, p. 352.
11. "Principles of Criticism," *The Prose of Edward Rowland Sill* (Boston and New York, 1900), p. 158.
12. *The Spirit of Modern Philosophy*, p. 466.
13. *Ibid.*, p. 297.
14. *Ibid.*, pp. 297-98.
15. *Herbert Spencer: An Estimate and a Review* (New York, 1904), p. 117.
16. *The World and the Individual*, I 239.
17. *In the Spirit of William James*, pp. 23-28. This treatment

should be compared with the defense of Royce as a California philosopher in Daniel Robinson, *Crucial Ideas in Philosophy* (Boston, 1955), pp. 149-64. Royce himself compares James to a frontiersman in *William James and Other Essays on the Philosophy of Life* (New York, 1912), p. 22.

18. *The Thought and Character of William James,* I, 781, 785.
19. *Scribner's Magazine,* X (1891), 383.
20. "Autobiographical Sketch," pp. 128-29.
21. *The Thought and Character of William James,* I, 466, 766.
22. *A Pluralistic Universe* (New York, 1909), pp. 57-60.
23. George Santayana, *The Middle Span* (New York, 1945), p. 152.
24. *The Thought and Character of William James,* I, 674.
25. "Doubting and Working," *Fugitive Essays,* p. 335.
26. "Joseph Le Conte," p. 330.
27. *The Spirit of Modern Philosophy,* p. 102.
28. *Ibid.,* p. 250.
29. "Kant's Relation to Modern Philosophic Progress," *Journal of Speculative Philosophy,* XV (1881), 368.
30. "The Duties of Americans in the Present War," *The Hope of the Great Community,* p. 11; "The Destruction of the Lusitania,"*ibid.,* p. 16; "The First Anniversary of the Sinking of the Lusitania, "May 7th, 1916," *ibid.,* p. 98.
31. "The Hope of the Great Community," *ibid.,* p. 29.
32. *The Thought and Character of William James,* I, 779-80. See also *The Philosophy of Loyalty* (New York, 1908), preface, pp. x-xi.
33. The courses that Royce supervised are described by Benjamin Rand in "Philosophical Instruction in Harvard University from 1636 to 1906," *Harvard Graduates' Magazine,* XXXVII (1928), 301-3. See also Richard C. Cabot, "Josiah Royce as a Teacher," *The Philosophical Review,* XXV (1916), 466-72; Palmer, pp. 7-8.
34. "Autobiographical Sketch," p. 131.
35. Palmer,pp. 6-7.
36. *The Way out of Agnosticism* (New York, 1890), p. 19.
37. "Abbot's Scientific Theism," *Science,* VII (1886), 335-38.
38. "Dr. Abbot's 'Way out of Agnosticism.'" *International Journal of Ethics,* I (1890-91), 111.
39. *Ibid.,* pp. 99, 107, 112.
40. *Ibid.,* p. 105.
41. *A Public Appeal for Redress to the Corporation and Overseers of Harvard University: Professor Royce's Libel* (Boston, 1891), pp. 12, 15.
42. *A Public Remonstrance Addressed to the Board of Overseers of Harvard University: Is Not Harvard Responsible for the Conduct*

of Her Professors as well as of Her Students? (Boston, 1892), p. 12.

43. "Abbot against Royce," *The Nation,* LIII (1891), 372.

44. *Ibid.,* pp. 389-90.

45. *The Thought and Character of William James,* I, 818.

46. *Collected Essays and Reviews* (New York, 1920), pp. 467-69.

47. *Ibid.,* p. 481.

48. *A Pluralistic Universe,* p. 66.

49. *The Thought and Character of William James,* I, 810. See *ibid.,* pp. 422, 425, for Peirce's agreement with James on Royce as a system-builder.

50. *The World and the Individual,* I, 308.

51. *The Thought and Character of William James,* II, 437.

52. "The Eternal and the Practical," *The Philosophical Review,* XIII (1904), 131.

53. *Ibid.,* p. 133.

54. On the pro-Royce side: John E. Smith, *Royce's Social Infinite: The Community of Interpretation* (New York, 1950), pp. 47-54; James Harry Cotton, *Royce on the Human Self* (Cambridge, Mass., 1954), pp. 195-204. On the pro-James side: Ralph Barton Perry, *In the Spirit of William James,* pp. 30-34; John Dewey, "A Reply to Professor Royce's Critique of Instrumentalism," *The Philosophical Review,* XXI (1912), 69-81.

55. James said in 1893 that he would master the Roycean system, and then either defend or attack it. See *The Thought and Character of William James,* I, 799.

56. *Ibid.,* p. 813.

57. *William James and Other Essays on the Philosophy of Life,* pp. 3-48.

Chapter Three

1. *The World and the Individual,* II, 34.

2. Royce's perennial self-defense on the score of consistency may be followed in the famous prefaces to his books. The crities are divided about this. In favor: Gabriel Marcel, *Royce's Metaphysics,* tr. by Virginia and Gordon Ringer (Chicago, 1956), p. 147; Loewenberg, editor's introduction to *Fugitive Essays,* p. 10; Palmer, pp. 5-6; Cotton, p. 321. Against: John H. Muirhead, *The Platonic Tradition in Anglo-Saxon Philosophy* (London, 1931), p. 350; G. Watts Cunningham, *The Idealistic Argument in Recent British and American Philosophy* (New York, 1933), pp. 257-60; W. H. Werkmeister, *A History of Philosophical Ideas in America* (New York, 1949), pp. 159-60; George Dykhuizen, *The Conception of God in the Philosophy of Josiah Royce* (Chicago, 1936), pp. 62-63.

3. *The Spirit of Modern Philosophy,* Preface, p. viii.
4. *Ibid.,* p. 138.
5. *Lectures on Modern Idealism,* p. 18.
6. "Kant's Relation to Modern Philosophic Progress," p. 377. See also *The World and the Individual,* I, 406-13.
7. *The Spirit of Modern Philosophy,* p. 127.
8. *The Religious Aspect of Philosophy,* p. 322.
9. *The Spirit of Modern Philosophy,* p. 139.
10. *The World and the Individual,* II, 145.
11. "On Purpose in Thought," *Fugitive Essays,* p. 259.
12. "Tests of Right and Wrong," *Ibid.,* pp. 215-16.
13. *Lectures on Modern Idealism,* p. 36.
14. *The Spirit of Modern Philosophy,* p. 201.
15. *Lectures on Modern Idealism,* p. 100.
16. *The Spirit of Modern Philosophy,* p. 158.
17. *The World and the Individual,* II, 41.
18. "Mind and Reality," p. 44.
19. *The Spirit of Modern Philosophy,* p. 151.
20. "Some Relations between Philosophy and Science in the First Half of the Nineteenth Century in Germany," Science, XXXVIII (1913), 571.
21. *Ibid.,* p. 576.
22. *The Spirit of Modern Philosophy,* p. 213.
23. *Ibid.,* p. 212. See also *Studies in Good and Evil,* introduction, pp. vi-vii.
24. *The Spirit of Modern Philosophy,* p. 395.
25. *Ibid.,* p. 226.
26. *Ibid.,* p. 266.
27. *Lectures on Modern Idealism,* p. 70.
28. 'The Implications of Self-consciousness," *Studies in Good and Evil,* p. 141.
29. *Studies in Good and Evil, Introduction,* pp. x, xi.
30. "Report of the Committee on Apparitions and Haunted Houses," *Proceedings of the American Society for Psychical Research,* I-IV (1885-1889), 229.
31. "A New Study of Psychology," *The International Journal of Ethics,* I (1891), 167.
32. *The World and the Individual,* II, 57.
33. *Royce's Metaphysics,* p. 41.
34. "Systematic Philosophy in America in the Years 1893, 1894 and 1895," *Archiv für Systematische Philosophie,* III (1897), 249.
35. *Royce's Logical Essays,* ed. by Daniels S. Robinson (Dubuque, Ia., 1951), p. 5. There is a growing body of secondary material on Royce as logician. See Bertrand Russell, *Introduction to Mathematical*

Philosophy (London, 1919), pp. 80-81; C. I. Lewis, "Types of Order and the System Σ," *The Philosophical Review,* XXV (1916), 179-91; E. G. Spaulding, "Realistic Aspects of Royce's Logic," Ibid., pp. 137-49; Harold N. Lee, "Royce as Logician," *Tulane Studies in Philosophy,* IV (1955), 61-74; Richard Hocking, "The Influence of Mathematics on Royce's Metaphysics," *The Journal of Philosophy,* LIII (1956), 77-91; Cotton, pp. 157- 89.

36. *The Problem of Christianity,* II, 117. See also Peirce, *Collected Papers,* VIII, 88.

37. "The Concept of the Infinite," *Hibbert Journal,* I (1902), 33.

38. *The World and the Individual,* I, 504; "The Concept of the Infinite," pp. 26-28. Royce's map of England has generated a lot of comment. See Peirce, *Collected Papers,* VIII, 94-95; Santayana, *Character and Opinion in the United States,* pp. 84-85; A. E. Taylor, *Elements of Metaphysics* (New York, 1909), pp. 150-51.

39. "The Concept of the Infinite," p. 45.

40. *The World and the Individual.* I, 503.

41. *The Problem of Christianity,* II, 281. See also Loewenberg, introduction to *Fugitive Essays,* pp. 13-14, 25-29; Smith, pp. 32-34, 82-85.

42. *The Problem of Christianity,* II, 219.

43. *Royce's Metaphysics,* p. 124.

44. *Logical Essays,* p. 223. See also Cotton, pp. 171-77; Richard Hocking, pp. 85-86.

45. *Elements of Metaphysics,* pp. 150-51. See also William James, *Some Problems of Philosophy* (New York, 1911), p. 185. For a professional mathematician's objections to Dedekind's and Royce's theory of the infinite: Cassius J. Keyser, *The Human Worth of Rigorous Thinking* (New York, 1916), pp. 139-62; also Bertrand Russell, *Introduction to Mathematical Philosophy,* pp. 138-39.

46. *Collected Papers,* VIII, 80-81.

47. *The Spirit of Modern Philosophy,* p. 272.

48. *Logical Essays,* pp. 60-61.

49. *Ibid.,* pp. 261-62.

50. *Ibid.,* p. 254.

51. *Ibid.,* pp. 275-77.

52. *The World and the Individual,* I, 16.

53. *Ibid.,* pp. 16-17.

54. "The Principles of Logic," *The Encyclopaedia of the Philosophical Sciences,* tr. by Ethel Meyer (London, 1913), p. 121-22.

55. The philosophical literature devoted to this question is enormous. For a criticism of Hegel, see Bertrand Russell, *A History of Western Philosophy* (New York, 1945), pp. 743-46; for a criticism of Royce, Daniel J. Bronstein, "Royce's Philosophic Method," *The Philo-*

sophical Review, XLIII (1934), 471-82. The coherence theory of truth is defended by the most Roycean of contemporary logicians: Daniel S. Robinson, *The Principles of Reasoning* (New York, 1930), p. 371.

56. *The World and the Individual,* I, 111.
57. *Ibid.*, p. 137.
58. *Ibid.*, p. 80.
59. *Ibid.*, p. 83.
60. *Ibid.*, p. 194.
61. *Ibid.*, p. 260.
62. *Ibid.*, p. 358.
63. *Collected Papers,* VIII, 81.
64. J. Loewenberg, *Royce's Synoptic Vision* (Baltimore, 1955).
65. *The Spirit of Modern Philosophy,* p. 323.

Chapter Four

1. *The World and the Individual,* I, 22.
2. *Ibid.*, pp. 22-23.
3. *Ibid.*, p. 31.
4. *Ibid.*, pp. 304-5.
5. *Ibid.*, p. 36.
6. *Ibid.*, p. 339.
7. *The Religious Aspect of Philosophy,* p. 397.
8. *The Spirit of Modern Philosophy,* p. 370.
9. *The Religious Aspect of Philosophy,* p. 390.
10. *Ibid.*, p. 409.
11. *Ibid.*, p. 399.
12. *Ibid.*, p. 425.
13. *The Spirit of Modern Philosophy,* pp. 372-73.
14. *The World and the Individual,* II, 30.
15. *Ibid.*, p. 28.
16. *Ibid.*, p. 32.
17. *Ibid.*, p. 33.
18. "The Eternal and the Practical," pp. 131-32.
19. *The World and the Individual,* I, 455.
20. *The Conception of Immortality,* pp. 17-18.
21. *The World and the Individual,* I, 458.
22. *The Conception of Immortality,* pp. 38-39.
23. *The Conception of God,* p. 258.
24. *The Conception of Immortality,* p. 82.
25. *The World and the Individual,* I, 447.
26. *Ibid.*, p. 387.
27. *Ibid.*, p. 460.

28. *Ibid.*, II, 432.
29. *Ibid.*, I, 390.
30. *Ibid.*, II, 263.
31. *Ibid.*, p. 264.
32. "Some Observations on the Anomalies of Self-consciousness," *Studies in Good and Evil*, pp. 193-94.
33. *The Problem of Christianity*, I, 132.
34. *Ibid.*, II, 312.
35. *The World and the Individual*, I, 91.
36. *Ibid.*, p. 240.
37. *Ibid.*, II, 268.
38. *Ibid.*, p. 269.
39. *Ibid.*, pp. 275-87.
40. *Ibid.*, p. 133.
41. *Ibid.*, p. 135.
42. *Ibid.*, p. 451.
43. *Ibid.*, p. 447.
44. *Ibid.*, p. 445.
45. *The Conception of God*, p. 351.
46. *The Spirit of Modern Philosophy*, p. 386.
47. *Ibid.*, p. 400.
48. *Ibid.*, p. 389.
49. *Ibid.*, p. 411.
50. *Ibid.*, p. 397.
51. "The Implications of Self-consciousness," p. 168.
52. *The World and the Individual, II*, pp. 336-37.
53. *Ibid.*, p. 386.
54. "The Problem of Job," *Studies in Good and Evil*, p. 14.
55. *Ibid.*, p. 27.
56. *The World and the Individual*, II, p. 354.
57. *Ibid.*, p. 355.
58. *The Spirit of Modern Philosophy*, p. 460.
59. *Ibid.*, p. 440.
60. *The World and the Individual*, II, 593.
61. *The Philosophy of Loyalty*, p. 15.
62. *The Problem of Christianity*, I, Preface, xvii.
63. *The Philosophy of Loyalty*, pp. 16-17.
64. *Ibid.*, p. 196.
65. *Ibid.*, p. 131.
66. *The Problem of Christianity*, I, Preface, xvi.
67. *Ibid.*, p. 14.
68. *Ibid.*, p. 98.
69. *Ibid.*, p. 176.
70. *Ibid.*, p. 191.

71. *Ibid.*, p. 304.
72. *Ibid.*, p. 320.
73. *Ibid.*, II, 428.
74. *Ibid.*, I, Preface, xxvi.
75. Letter to Mary Whiton Calkins, *The Philosophical Review*, XXV (1916), 294.
76. *The Spirit of Modern Philosophy, Preface*, p. vi.
77. William James, *A Pluralistic Universe*, p. 296; George Santayana, *Character and Opinion in the United States*, p. 71; G. H. Howison, *The Conception of God*, pp. 98-99. See also Charles Renouvier, "Josiah Royce—le panthéisme idéaliste," *La Critique Philosophique*, IV (1888), 4-24, 85-120; John Dewey, review of *The World and the Individual, The Philosophical Review*, IX (1900), 310-23, XI (1902), 392-407; W. H. Werkmeister, *Philosophical Ideas in America*, pp. 138-40, 154-55, 158-59. For the defense: Josiah Royce, *The Conception of God*, pp. 328-37; Paul E. Johnson, "Josiah Royce: Theist or Pantheist?" *Harvard Theological Review*, XXI (1928), 197-205; Daniel S. Robinson, *Crucial Issues in Philosophy*, pp. 131-36; J. Loewenberg, *Royce's Synoptic Vision*, p. 16.
78. Douglas Clyle Macintosh, *The Problem of Knowledge*, p. 387; Ralph Barton Perry, *In the Spirit of William James*, p. 34; Hugh Joseph Tallon, *The Concept of Self in British and American Idealism* (Washington, D.C., 1939), pp. 42-49.
79. A. C. Ewing, *Idealism: A Critical Survey* (London, 1934), pp. 51-52; Arthur Kenyon Rogers, *English and American Philosophy since 1800* (New York, 1922), pp. 290-91; Addison Webster Moore, "Some Logical Aspects of Purpose." *Studies in Logical Theory*, ed. by John Dewey (Chicago, 1903), pp. 365-66. See also John Dewey, "Voluntarism in the Roycean Philosophy," *The Philosophical Review*, XXV (1916), 17-26; George Dykhuizen, *The Conception of God in the Philosophy of Josiah Royce* (Chicago, 1936), pp. 47-50; Cotton, pp. 105-6. For the defense: Brand Blanshard, *The Nature of Thought* (New York, 1940), I, 518-19.
80. William Ernest Hocking, *The Meaning of God in Human Experience* (New Haven, Conn., 1912), pp. 157-62.
81. Michael Cronin, *The Science of Ethics* (Dublin, 1930), I, 581-84; A. J. M. Milne, *The Social Philosophy of English Idealism* (London, 1962), pp. 305-6; H. B. Jefferson, "Royce on the Problem of Evil," *The Journal of Religion*, XI (1931), 360-61; Charles Hartshorne, "Royce's Mistake—and Achievement," *The Journal of Philosophy*, LIII (1956), 126. For the defense: A. E. Taylor, *Elements of Metaphysics*, p. 398; Marcel, pp. 70-76.
82. Walter Goodnow Everett, *Moral Values* (New York, 1918), pp. 45-49; W. H. Werkmeister, *Theories of Ethics* (Lincoln, Neb.,

1961), p. 433; Ralph Barton Perry, *The Present Conflict of Ideals* (New York, 1919), pp. 267-71. For the defense: Moses Judah Aronson, *La Philosophie morale de Josiah Royce* (Paris, 1927), pp. 149-62; René Le Senne, *Traité de morale générale* (Paris, 1942), pp. 534-35, 653-54; Cotton, pp. 243-45.

Selected Bibliography

BIBLIOGRAPHIES

BURR, NELSON R. *A Critical Bibliography of Religion in America* (Princeton University Press, 1961), pp. 1119-21.

LOEWENBERG, J. "A Bibliography of the Unpublished Writings of Josiah Royce," *The Philosophical Review,* XXVI (1917), 578-82.

RAND, BENJAMIN. "A Bibliography of the Writings of Josiah Royce," *The Philosophical Review,* XXV (1916), 515-22.

PRIMARY SOURCES

Primer of Logical Analysis for the Use of Composition Students. San Francisco: Bancroft, 1881.

The Religious Aspect of Philosophy. Boston and New York: Houghton, Mifflin, 1885.

California from the Conquest in 1846 to the Second Vigilance Committee in San Francisco: A Study of American Character. Boston and New York: Houghton, Mifflin, 1886.

The Feud of Oakfield Creek: A Novel of California Life. Boston and New York: Houghton, Mifflin, 1887.

The Spirit of Modern Philosophy. Boston and New York: Houghton, Mifflin, 1892.

The Conception of God: A Philosophical Discussion concerning the Nature of the Divine Idea as a Demonstrable Reality, with Joseph Le Conte, G. H. Howison, and Sidney Edward Mezes. New York: Macmillan, 1897.

Studies in Good and Evil: A Series of Essays upon Problems of Philosophy and Life. New York: Appleton, 1898. The titles in this volume are the following: "The Problem of Job," "The Case of John Bunyan," "Tennyson and Pessimism," "The Knowledge of Good and Evil," "Natural Law, Ethics and Evolution," "The Anomalies of Self-consciousness," "The Implications of Self-consciousness," "Self-consciousness, Social Consciousness and Nature," "Originality and Consciousness," "Meister Eckhart," "An Episode of Early California Life: The Squatter Riot of 1850 in Sacramento," and "Jean Marie Guyau."

The World and the Individual, First Series: The Four Historical Conceptions of Being. New York: Macmillan, 1899.

The Conception of Immortality. Boston and New York: Houghton, Mifflin, 1900.

The World and the Individual, Second Series: Nature, Man, and the Moral Order. New York: Macmillan, 1901.

Herbert Spencer: An Estimate and a Review. New York: Fox, Duffield, 1904.

Outlines of Psychology. New York: Macmillan, 1906.

Race Questions, Provincialism, and Other American Problems. New York: Macmillan, 1908.

The Philosophy of Loyalty. New York: Macmillan, 1908.

William James and Other Essays on the Philosophy of Life. New York: Macmillan, 1911. The titles in this volume are the following: "William James and the Philosophy of Life," "Loyalty and Insight," "What is Vital in Christianity?" "The Problem of Truth in the Light of Recent Discussion," and "Immortality."

The Sources of Religious Insight. New York: Scribner's, 1912.

The Problem of Christianity. New York: Macmillan, 1913.

War and Insurance. New York: Macmillan, 1914.

The Hope of the Great Community. New York: Macmillan, 1916. The titles in this volume are the following: "The Duties of Americans in the Present War," "The Destruction of the Lusitania," "The Hope of the Great Community," "The Possibility of International Insurance," "The First Anniversary of the Sinking of the Lusitania, May 7th, 1916," and "Autobiographical Sketch: Words of Professor Royce at the Walton Hotel at Philadelphia, December 29, 1915."

Lectures on Modern Idealism. Ed. by J. Loewenberg. Yale University Press, 1919.

Fugitive Essays. Ed. by J. Loewenberg. Cambridge: Harvard University Press, 1920. The titles in this volume are the following: "Schiller's Ethical Studies," "Shelley and the Revolution," "The Nature of Voluntary Progress," "The Practical Significance of Pessimism," "Pessimism and Modern Thought," "Tests of Right and Wrong," "On Purpose in Thought." "George Eliot as a Religious Teacher," "Natural Rights and Spinoza's Essay on Liberty," "The Decay of Earnestness," "Doubting and Working," "How Beliefs are Made," "A Neglected Study," "The Problem of Paracelsus," and "Pope Leo's Philosophical Movement and Its Relation to Modern Thought."

The Social Philosophy of Josiah Royce. Ed. by Stuart Gerry Brown. Syracuse: Syracuse University Press, 1950. The titles in this volume are the following: "Race Questions and Prejudices,"

"Provincialism," "The Nature and Need of Loyalty," "Individualism," "Loyalty to Loyalty," "Conscience," "Some American Problems in their Relation to Loyalty," "The Hope of the Great Community," "Address on War and Insurance," and "The Possibility of International Insurance."

Royce's Logical Essays. Ed. by Daniel S. Robinson. Dubuque, Ia.: William C. Brown, 1951. The titles in this volume are the following: "Recent Logical Inquiries and their Psychological Bearings," "The Mechanical, the Historical and the Statistical," "The Problem of Truth in the Light of Recent Discussion," "Error and Truth," "Axiom," "Individual," "Mind," "Negation," "Order," "Definitions and Debates," "Introductory Note to Enriques' Problems of Science," "Hypotheses and Leading Ideas," "Introduction to Poincaré's Foundations of Science," "Benno Erdmann's Logic," and "An Extension of the Algebra of Logic."

The Religious Philosophy of Josiah Royce. Ed. by Stuart Gerry Brown. Syracuse: Syracuse University Press, 1952. The titles in this volumes are: "The Possibility of Error," "Individuality and Freedom," "The Temporal and the Eternal," "The Conception of Immortality," "Loyalty and Religion," "The Idea of the Universal Community," "The Moral Burden of the Individual," "The Realm of Grace," "Time and Guilt," and "Atonement."

SECONDARY SOURCES

ARONSON, MOSES JUDAH. *La Philosophie morale de Josiah Royce* Paris: Presses Universitaires de France, 1927. A favorable description of Royce's ethical theories.

BAKEWELL, CHARLES M. "Royce as an Interpreter of American Ideals," *International Journal of Ethics,* XXVII (1917), 306-16. An article on Royce's practice of arguing from ethics to metaphysics.

BIXLER, JULIUS. "Josiah Royce—Twenty Years After," *Harvard Theological Review,* XXIX (1936), 197-224. A defense of Roycean absolutism as a background for a religious synthesis of experience and thought, intellect and will, God and the world.

BRONSTEIN, D. J. "Royce's Philosophic Method," *The Philosophical Review,* XLIII (1934), 471-82. An argument that Royce's use of the principle of contradiction is vitiated by his surreptitious introduction of premises that need not be accepted.

BUCKHAM, JOHN WRIGHT. "The Contribution of Professor Royce to Christian Thought," *Harvard Theological Review,* VIII (1915), 219-37. An argument that Royce's theology can be given a sound Pauline interpretation.

CLELAND, ROBERT GLASS. Introduction to the reprint of *California*. New York: Knopf, 1948, pp. ix-xxx. A favorable discussion of Royce as historican.

COTTON, JAMES HARRY. *Royce on the Human Self*. Cambridge: Harvard University Press, 1954. The best general introduction to Royce's philosophy.

CUNNINGHAM, G. WATTS. *The Idealist Argument in Recent British and American Philosophy*. New York: Century 1933. A treatise that devotes much space to Royce, and searches acutely for fallacies in his theory of ideas.

DEWEY, JOHN. "A Reply to Professor Royce's Critique of Instrumentalism," *The Philosophical Review*, XXI (1912), 69-81. A denial that Royce is correct in saying that the instrumentalist definition of truth leads logically to absolute idealism.

DYKHUIZEN, GEORGE. *The Conception of God in the Philosophy of Josiah Royce*. Chicago: Chicago University Press, 1936. A systematic negative criticism of Royce's idealism, voluntarism, and absolutism.

EWING, A. C. *Idealism: A Critical Survey*. London: Methuen, 1934. A treatise that allots a high place to Royce even while dissenting from his system.

HOCKING, RICHARD. "Royce Forty Years Later," *The Review of Metaphysics*, X (1956), 64-72. A brief but helpful review of some of the recent literature on Royce.

HOCKING, WILLIAM ERNEST. "The Ontological Argument in Royce and Others." *Contemporary Idealism in America*. Ed. by Clifford Barrett. New York: Macmillan, 1932. A defense of Royce against Santayana on the relation between essence and existence.

HOWISON, G. H. "The City of God, and the True God as Its Head." *The Conception of God*, with Royce, Le Conte, and Mezes (New York: Macmillan, 1897), pp. 81-132. A basic criticism of Royce's absolutism by an idealist who considered it to be monism and pantheism.

In Memoriam: Josiah Royce, Born November 20, 1855, The Journal of Philosophy, LIII (1956), 57-139. Estimations of Royce, mainly favorable, commemorating the centenary of his birth.

JAMES, WILLIAM. *A Pluralistic Universe*. New York: Longmans, Green, 1909. A defense of a philosophy that contradicts and condemns Royce's.

———. "The Religious Aspect of Philosophy." *Collected Essays and Reviews*. New York: Longmans, Green, 1920. As favorable a verdict on Royce as James ever made, but with references to Hegelianism and monism that foreshadow the coming "Battle of the Absolute."

JEFFERSON, H. B. "Royce on the Problem of Evil," *Journal of Religion,* XI (1931), 359-77. An argument that Royce is wrong because evil cannot be experienced by God and man in any comparable manner.

JOHNSON, PAUL E. "Josiah Royce: Theist or Pantheist?" *Harvard Theological Review,* XXI (1928), 197-205. The answer is that Royce is a theist.

KEYSER, CASSIUS J. "The Axiom of Infinity: A New Presupposition of Thought." *The Human Worth of Rigorous Thinking.* Columbia University Press, 1916. A mathematician's negative criticism of Royce's theory of the infinite.

LEE, HAROLD N. "Royce as Logician," *Tulane Studies in Philosophy,* IV (1955), 61-74. A brief but important analysis of Royce's logic.

LE SENNE, RENE. *Traité de morale générale.* Paris: Presses Universitaires de France, 1942. A massive treatise on ethics, interesting to the student of Royce because of the passing references to him by a notable French thinker.

LOEWENBERG, J. "Editor's Introduction." *Fugitive Essays.* Cambridge: Harvard University Press, 1920. A good, although too uncritical, guide to Royce's philosophy by way of his early essays.

———. *Royce's Synoptic Vision.* Baltimore: Johns Hopkins Press, 1955. A favorable essay on major themes in Royce's philosophy.

McCREARY, JOHN. "The Religious Philosophy of Josiah Royce," *Journal of Religion,* XXX (1950), 117-31. A history of Royce's theological ideas as they developed book by book.

MACINTOSH, DOUGLAS CLYDE. *The Problem of Knowledge.* New York: Macmillan, 1915. A general treatise by a contemporary of Royce who criticizes his philosophy from the standpoint of pragmatism.

MARCEL, GABRIEL. *Royce's Metaphysics.* Tr. by Virginia and Gordon Ringer. Chicago: Regnery, 1956. The best critical analysis of Royce by his peer among philosophers.

MEAD, G. H. "The Philosophies of Royce, James, and Dewey in Their American Setting," *International Journal of Ethics,* XL (1929-30), 211-31. A parallel study, the upshot of which is that Dewey remains the most American of the three thinkers; Royce, the most Europeanized.

MILNE, A. J. M. *The Social Philosophy of English Idealism.* London: Allen and Unwin, 1962. An extensive monograph that "places" Royce in recent philosophy and argues for a basic contradiction between his metaphysics and his ethics.

MONSMAN, DIANA. "Royce's Conception of Experience and of the Self," *The Philosophical Review,* XLIX (1940), 325-45. A criticism of Royce that finds inconsistencies too easily in definitions taken out of context.

MONTAGUE, WILLIAM PEPERELL. *The Ways of Knowing*. London: Allen and Unwin, 1925. The dialogue in this volume is a dialectical exercise in which the objective idealist speaks for Royce.

MOORE, ADDISON WEBSTER. "Some Logical Aspects of Purpose." *Studies in Logical Theory*. Ed. by John Dewey. Chicago: Chicago University Press, 1903. A closely reasoned argument that Royce's theory of ideas is incoherent.

MUIRHEAD, JOHN H. *The Platonic Tradition in Anglo-Saxon Philosophy*. London: Allen and Unwin, 1931 A history of idealism with a long, useful, fair, analysis of Royce's thought.

NEVINS, ALLEN. *Frémont, Pathmaker of the West*. New York: Appleton-Century, 1939. A biography that does not accept Royce's hostile account of the subject.

PALMER, GEORGE HEBERT. "In Dedication: Josiah Royce," *Contemporary Idealism in America*, ed. by Clifford Barrett (New York: Macmillan, 1932), pp. 1-9. An affectionate memoir about Royce as man and teacher by one of his Harvard colleagues.

Papers in Honor of Josiah Royce on His Sixtieth Birthday. Ed. by J. E. Creighton, *The Philosophical Review*, XXV (1916), 229-522. Judgments on Royce, pro and con, by his contemporaries in philosophy.

PERRY, RALPH BARTON. "Professor Royce's Refutation of Realism and Pluralism," *The Monist*, XII (1902), 446-58. A condemnation of Royce on the ground that he misrepresents the position of the realist.

———. *The Thought and Character of William James*. Boston: Little, Brown, 1935. A magisterial source book of documents and critical introductions, of which three central chapters are devoted to the relations between James and Royce.

———. "Two American Philosophers: William James and Josiah Royce." *In the Spirit of William James* New Haven: Yale University Press, 1938. An enlightening parallel study of the two philosophers.

RAMSEY, PAUL. "The Idealistic View of Moral Evil: Josiah Royce and Bernard Bosanquet," *Philosophy and Phenomenological Research*, VI (1946), 554-89. A defense of the two thinkers, once their absolute idealism has been reformulated as absolute theism.

RAND, BENJAMIN. "Philosophical Instruction in Harvard University from 1636 to 1906," *Harvard Graduates Magazine*, XXXVII (1928), 296-311. A chronicle that itemizes the courses allotted to Royce.

RENOUVIER, CHARLES. "Josiah Royce—le panthéisme idéaliste," *La Critique Philosophique,* IV (1888), 4-24, 85-120. A long critical analysis of *The Religious Aspect of Philosophy* that rejects the systematic argument but praises the spirit of the writer and his handling of specific subjects.

ROBINSON, DANIEL S. *Crucial Issues in Philosophy.* Boston: Christopher Publishing House, 1955. A defense of idealism in general and of Royce in particular.

ROGERS, ARTHUR KENYON. *English and American Philosophy since 1800.* New York: Macmillan, 1922. A history with a chapter very critical of Royce.

ROYCE, SARAH. *A Frontier Lady: Recollections of the Gold Rush and Early California.* Ed. by Ralph Henry Gabriel. New Haven: Yale University Press, 1932. Royce's mother's account of the family trek across the continent.

SANTAYANA, GEORGE. "Josiah Royce." *Character and Opinion in the United States.* New York: Scribner's, 1920. An unsympathetic discussion of Royce by a pupil and a philosopher too committed to a different kind of philosophy to do him justice.

SMITH, JOHN E. *Royce's Social Infinite: The Community of Interpretation.* New York: Liberal Arts Press, 1950. An able exposition and defense of the final phase of Royce's philosophy.

SORLEY, W. R. "Josiah Royce, 1855-1916," *Proceedings of the British Academy, 1915-1916,* pp. 585-92. An appreciative obituary by an important philosopher contemporary with Royce.

TALLON, HUGH JOSEPH. *The Concept of Self in British and American Idealism.* Washington, D.C.: Catholic University of America Press, 1939. A monograph with a negative criticism of Royce from the standpoint of Thomism.

TAYLOR, A. E. *Elements of Metaphysics.* New York: Macmillan, 1909. A treatise that criticizes Royce incidentally from the standpoint of a somewhat different form of idealism.

WERKMEISTER, W. H. *A History of Philosophical Ideas in America.* New York: Ronald Press, 1949. A textbook with a good analytical chapter on Royce.

WIEMAN, HENRY NELSON and BERNARD EUGENE MELAND. *American Philosophies of Religion.* New York: Willett, Clark, 1936. A general history of the subject with a few descriptive pages on Royce.

WRIGHT, WILLIAM KELLEY. *A History of Modern Philosophy.* New York: Macmillan, 1941. A textbook with an easy, simplified account of Royce's system.

Index

Index